Colin Woods

BARBEL AND ROACH BY CHOICE

Mereo Books

2nd Floor, 6-8 Dyer Street, Cirencester, Gloucestershire, GL7 2PF
An imprint of Memoirs Publishing www.mereobooks.com

BARBEL AND ROACH BY CHOICE: 978-1-86151-938-2

First published in Great Britain in 2019
by Mereo Books, an imprint of Memoirs Publishing

The address for Memoirs Publishing Group Limited can be
found at www.memoirspublishing.com

The Memoirs Publishing Group Ltd Reg. No. 7834348

Typeset in 9/12pt Bembo
by Wiltshire Associates Ltd.
Printed and bound in Great Britain

BARBEL AND ROACH BY CHOICE

CONTENTS

Preface

Dedication

About the author

Acknowledgements

BARBEL

Days by the water in pursuit of big fish

ROACH

THIS WAS A WORLD OF...
SHEER COMPULSION
SHEER ENJOYMENT
SHEER CONTENTMENT

TOTAL FISHING... PURE ANGLING

PREFACE

⌒∘⌒

The drive to the river was merely a means to an end. Little pleasure was to be had amidst the busy, busy traffic with the omnipresent tailgater. There was little chance to glance towards the water meadows or the adjacent hedgerows housing a variety of birds and wildlife, just oncoming cars to watch out for. But the click-click of the indicators told me that an escape from the rat race was imminent, and warranted a smile. The quiet country lane lacked traffic and the view of rich green fields and grazing livestock was there to be enjoyed.

As I turned from the road onto a track, I felt my mood soar. The fishery I was heading for was one of a few that gave me a real buzz of excitement on arrival, the sort of feeling all the carpers must have experienced as they neared Redmire Pool in its glory days. But here there were big barbel and roach and good dace, chub, pike, carp and grayling to be caught. There were few rules to comply with, only that night fishing was not allowed and the first to arrive had to open the gate and the last to leave to close it. Today it was closed, so I knew I would have the fishery to myself. My spirits soared further.

The excitement continued on the bankside as I headed for a favoured swim. In reality there was no guarantee of catching a good barbel or roach, but most days the landing net would at least be dampened by a nice chub. Nice? They were big - four, five and possibly six-pounders. In fishing every day is regarded as a success, for today, tomorrow or next week a big fish will bring joy and that joy will not be ephemeral but apportioned to every visit.

Success was down to approach, stealth and getting it right, but above all serendipity. This was a world of sheer compulsion, sheer enjoyment, sheer contentment; total fishing, pure angling.

In memory of Derek Johnson, who died far too young. He was both a brilliant stillwater trout and pike angler and a keen barbel enthusiast. Derek was as good an angler as any other and a true mate, and this book is dedicated to him.

ABOUT THE AUTHOR

⟶∘⟵

Born in Perivale, Middlesex, Colin Woods discovered the joys of float fishing for roach on a local canal at the tender age of five. After joining a local club, he widened his angling experience to the Thames, Great Ouse, Kentish Stour and Hampshire Avon. A quick learner, he began collecting trophies in angling competitions while he was still at school. In his late teens he joined a specimen group and started targeting the bigger fish, developing a particular interest in barbel and roach.

During his career in local government, dealing with the rivers of London, Colin won a medal for his contribution to the completion of the Thames Barrier. Later he left his job and moved south to be near his beloved Hampshire Avon, working in local conservation and accounts offices and doing freelance photographic and feature work for angling magazines.

Colin has written many articles for clubs such as the Barbel Catchers and features for the angling press, as well as providing illustrations for books and magazines. Now retired, he enjoys swimming in the nearby sea, whose therapeutic qualities help to relieve the rheumatic pains which have threatened to curtail his fishing time. He still spends long hours on the bank hunting for the next large roach or specimen barbel.

ACKNOWLEDGEMENTS

My biggest thank you has to go to Jennifer Phippard, who has helped me immensely with this book. I don't think I could have completed it without her help. Not only has she typed out some of my manuscript, which I could barely read myself at times, she has drawn some of the sketches.

Digital technology is not my strong point, and at times I have felt like throwing my laptop out of the window when I have got stuck on something, but Jennifer has always sorted out the many problems as well as showing me how to use my printer, which could be an Enigma machine for all I know.

Jennifer, who owns a local driving school, is an author herself, having written a number of children's books.

I have to thank those who encouraged me to write to begin with. They weren't anglers, just people I worked with who thought I should express my passion for angling in written form. I am indebted for their persuasion.

Over the years I have met hundreds of anglers of different character; some fanatical, literally living on the bankside for months on end, others more casual in their commitment, and I have been greatly inspired by their shared enthusiasm to go fishing. Many have their own style of angling, some are more successful than others, but what they have in common is their love of the art of angling and their willingness to share their knowledge and experience. I've always tried to learn from my own experiences and forethought, but undoubtedly much of my knowledge is the result of what I have learnt from others. Had I not become an angler I would never have met all those great characters, and it is hard to imagine how empty life would have been without them. A huge 'thank you' to all for having enriched my life.

All pictures are by the author except where otherwise stated.

INTRODUCTION

This is my first book. I have written the odd short story before, but nothing intended for publication, although I have written reviews for angling publications of tackle I have tested and books I have read, and articles for club magazines.

The intention of this book is to reminisce over past experiences and how my approach and angling styles have evolved over the years, hopefully in an interesting manner. It also aims to explain how I fish nowadays for barbel and roach, the tackle and bait I use and the terminal rigs employed.

Although I have written in an off-the-cuff style, I have given a lot of thought to the content and structure, which has taken a great deal of time. I have a number of books on barbel and roach in my collection as well as general angling books which have chapters devoted to the two species. Whilst writing I deliberately avoided referring to the content of these books, although I know one or two of them very well. I have referred to them only to confirm the Nottingham/Wallis cast in the Lonsdale Library title *Fine Angling for Coarse Fish*, dated 1930 (it is somewhat amusing to see it explained with pictures), and to check the shotting pattern advised by L. A. Parker in his book "This Fishing". No doubt at some time in the future I will re-read some of my books and discover points I have neglected and issues that are contrary to mine. For a while I've had a reprint of Greville Fennell's *The Book of the Roach*, dated 1870, which I will read with interest once I have put my pen down.

My thoughts on angling race away in my mind, but my pen is much slower in putting them on paper. They are my thoughts, and others may well disagree in some ways. I have tried the best I can to accurately give details of names, catches and descriptive accounts. Possibly, in some cases, the odd mistake has been made, for which I can only apologise.

I have tried to structure this book in an interesting way. Generally most chapters reflect chronological events. The 'Then and Now' chapter captures how expectations have been realised through experience and endeavour. All my stories from the riverbank are totally true, with the exception of the odd name which has been changed where appropriate. The 'Let's go fishing' and 'Digby calls' tales may contain an element of poetic licence.

I have always taken my fishing seriously, and I tend to be elusive at times; I disappear into a different world on the bank, deep in thought about my objectives and what is the most pragmatic approach.

The absorption is total at times, for to me angling is the ultimate form of pleasure. On the other hand, I am fully aware that there are aspects of fishing that should be fun. I am equally content to take time out cheerily catching a few small roach, crucians or tench or whatever dips my float on a scenic local pond. Often I will enjoy the company of friends or guests on the riverbank or lakeside, having a softly-spoken chat and reflecting on the day's fishing at the end of the day over a pint and a meal at home or a cup of tea in a local pub.

Over the years I have read quite a number of articles and books on angling, some vintage, others modern. I've always tended to question what has been written – does it sound logical or is it nonsensical? Sometimes, in the articles I have written, I have made bold statements which I believed to be true. With barbel, the late Fred Crouch, a renowned River Lea and Royalty Fishery angler, used to phone me sometimes about what I had written, asking me to explain my thoughts. At least he never appeared to disagree with me.

In this book I may well have given opinions which may not be totally correct, and I would expect the reader to question my reasoning as I have done of others.

Old books make great reading, not only from an entertaining, nostalgic point of view but because the contents, although of less relevance these days, may be thought-provoking and have modern-day applications.

There are many recently-published books on barbel and a few on roach. Most are good, but two classics from the twentieth century spring to mind. My favourite barbel book has to be Peter Wheat's *The Fighting Barbel*. I've had the pleasure of meeting

Some of the author's collection of books on barbel

Roach literature

Peter, a well-respected life-long barbel angler, who I believe is now the president of the Barbel Society. His book is very informative, and when it was published it was far in advance of anything previously written about barbel.

The roach classic has to be Captain L.A. Parker's *This Fishing*, first published in 1948. It is not entirely about roach, but the emphasis is very much on the Hampshire Avon, and in particular the redfin. One remarkable section has a record not only of the air and water temperature for every day of the year but also the air pressure and fishing conditions – hugely interesting. Some of the areas fished by 'the Skipper' on the Avon are familiar to me, which makes it even more interesting.

My book may differ in part from others; it is not intended to do so, it merely reflects my viewpoint and methodology. My approach is candid, and I trust it is worth the read. Before writing about the characteristics of barbel and roach, as well as giving information about tackle and approach and offering my own personal tips and advice, I would like to take you on river trips for both species. Firstly I'll go back in time to get a flavour of my early memories, which may have resulted in lesser specimens but were equally adventurous and inspirational.

HOW IT ALL BEGAN

A ngling has been my lifelong passion. I first fished as a five or six-year-old with my brother, mother and aunt on my local canal and developed a keen interest in the art of angling some five years later, as I will explain in another chapter. I could identify the fish I caught at that early age and roach were my favourite, though I doubt if I could have spelt the word back then, in my first year at infant school.

The compulsion to fish in my teenage years must have been an inherent one and I had an insatiable hunger to catch anything with fins. That compulsion has never left me. Later on I was able to pinpoint which species I wanted to catch and where from.

By my late teens I had fished many rivers and stillwaters, but my choice of venue was much dependent upon accessibility; I was reliant upon how far I could cycle, where the club coach visited or where others could take me by car. I had won a place at university to take a degree in Geology, but having already worked all through earlier summer holidays to pay for my keep, the thought of having to do the same for the next three years was unappealing. My friends who were working had money in their pockets and more freedom, so I simply had to get a full-time job.

Luckily, after a couple of interviews I did get a job, in local government. The pay was low to start with, but there was the certainty of annual increments with long service, plus the all-important bonus of good holiday entitlement. Initially I was posted to Kew, and then transferred to Westminster and Waterloo, where I spent the remainder of my career with the authority. Fortunately promotions came my way and mostly I worked in finance, dealing with contract payments relating to river and refuse disposal projects. My small claim to fame was making the largest ever single payment made by a local authority, in addition to indirectly providing the PM with expenditure details for Prime Minister's question time.

Not long after I started work I could afford a cheap car. It was not a very good one, but I have never forgotten the freedom it gave me to get out on the road and fish wherever I wanted. It was a strange feeling unloading the tackle from the car for the first time by a Colne Valley pit and returning home with damp hands on the steering wheel, having washed bream slime off me. The car liked oil more than it did petrol, and after four months its engine had just about expired, so I sold it, remarkably making a profit on it. A slightly newer car followed, which could take me further afield. The world was my oyster, or more pertinently barbel and roach were, or whatever I wanted to fish for.

Around that time there was already a proliferation of specimen-hunting groups, and finding I had an intense passion to catch better fish, I joined the Surrey Specimen Group. Individually we fished for different species, carp, chub, barbel and roach, but we shared the same common commitment to

catching bigger fish. It was a joy to meet young, like-minded anglers like myself. The main ethos shared by all of us was to fish with stealth, something I have tried to adhere to ever since, though there has been the odd lapse at times. Colour mattered and clothing had to be green; if it wasn't, it was dyed. Tackle too had to be green, and if it wasn't, it was painted green, whether it was rods, reels (even bale arms) or rod rests. Everything had to be green. Movement on the bank had to be surreptitious and bankside cover had

Anglers should make use of bankside cover at all times. Colour and stealth matter.

to be used to advantage whenever possible. I made good friends with some of the members of the group as well as those of other groups I had contact with. We fished many times together for a good number of years. We caught some good fish too between us, including a tench caught by Pete Pilley which would have been a new record at the time but for some weight loss prior to an official weighing.

I consider myself an all-round angler. Whilst I do have a particular affinity for barbel and roach, I have fished for many other species over the years, notably chub, tench, carp, pike, grayling and trout, all of which have given me a great understanding of the habits of fish and the approach needed to succeed in angling. Fish for one species and likely you will become stale and dogmatic; much can be learnt from the various techniques of fishing for other species. Just look how match and carp anglers have learnt from one another. Although the Thames, Kennet and Hampshire Avon have been my favourite rivers, I have fished further afield, as far as the Annan in Scotland for chub, the Fens and Norfolk Broads for pike mostly and Ireland on a couple of occasions for tench and pike. My heart does lie with the Hampshire Avon and its barbel and roach. It is my home ground; all other waters are away fixtures.

As my career in local government was coming to an end, having already moved to Surrey, I moved again to Christchurch, whilst I could still get a mortgage. Commuting a hundred miles each way every day wasn't my idea of fun, but eventually redundancy followed. Work wasn't easy to come by on the south coast. I did find a couple of jobs, but both soon ended in redundancy. It was becoming a habit.

Living in Christchurch meant I had to give up one of my other interests, which was watching some of the home games of my favourite football club, Brentford FC, a great, friendly club, which I still closely follow.

Photography has always been another hobby, though at times, it has been a little too expensive for me to fully kit myself out. Eventually, after having a number of photos published, I undertook some photographic work for *Anglers' Mail* and *Coarse Angling* magazines, as well as writing the odd tackle or book review. A few years back I unfortunately developed a troublesome neck condition which hampered my fishing, but at least it gave me some free time to complete this book. Today I spend much of my time on the bankside just taking pictures. A full kit is still expensive, but I'm getting there.

I am also keen on cryptic crosswords and have been one of the winners of the Saturday *Daily Telegraph* prize crossword, a number of years ago. My other interest is art. I went to art school in my spare time when at college and I've always been keen on line drawings and painting, though I've never been able to devote enough time to it.

My Christchurch home has become a bit of an anglers' retreat for a number of barbel fishers. All have been welcome, and I have enjoyed many a laugh and a conversation over a pint. I trust my advice has been of some worth. I've had the good fortune of meeting many fine anglers on the riverbank, and some have become good friends. Each has their own style of fishing and all catch good fish - that is just a reflection of the fact that angling is not an exact science, it is all about conviction.

There have been diversions along my portentous motorway of life. One junction took me in the direction of an autobahn in fact, which ultimately ended in a Bavarian alpine village, where I met my partner, a blonde Fraülein called Uschi. Over the years I have been a member of many angling clubs as well as specialist groups, most notably the Barbel Catchers' Club, of which I was a member for several years.

Back in the day, a Barbel Catchers fish-in on the Royalty. Back row: Dave Street, Steve Carden, the late Chris Wild, Trefor West, Mike Rice, Mike Stevens, Mick Nicholls, the late Tony Miles, Colin Woods. In front: Phil Glossop. It is with great sadness that I add that my old friend Mike Rice has recently passed away.

The amiable Dave Magson on the Hampshire Avon

Steve Smith playing a winter barbel on the Dorset Stour during a BCC fish-in

THEN AND NOW

Let's go back to the 1960s. I was fourteen years old, and although the canal I was fishing was in suburbia, the outlook was far from urban. Its watery ribbon followed the contours of the lower slopes of a wooded hill, an eminence rising to over 270 feet above sea level, one of the highest in the area. Mature trees fringed the opposite bank, interspersed with grassy glades. On my bank the cindered towpath continued endlessly in both directions. Behind me, the fence panels marking the boundaries of gardens gave little indication of human presence.

My favoured spot was very familiar to me, as I had fished there many times before, the attraction being that it was only a five-minute bike ride from home. Roach were the target; I'd caught a good few on previous visits. I liked the look of the fish, fins red in colour with variegated green to white flanks. They were not of great size compared to their river cousins, but big enough. The canal also held quite a few gudgeon and some nice perch. Bream were mostly confined to an area further along the bank and there was the occasional carp, though I never caught or saw one myself.

The tackle was simple: a bamboo pole with a short line leading to a small porcupine float, a couple of shot and a size 16 hook completing the rig. As usual maggots were the bait. After two or three hours I'd caught a few roach and gudgeon, and the sun was beginning to set. A few maggots remained in the bait tin, most of which had turned into casters, which were thrown in for attraction.

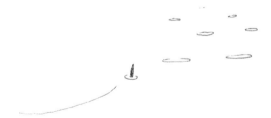

Small rings began to appear around the float, suggesting surface-feeding fish, so I removed the shot, applied some grease to the line, and baited with a single caster. The float immediately flew away and I was into a better fish, a much bigger roach and noticeably richer in colour. Several more followed, again all much of a larger size and superior in condition; beautiful fish. The light began to fade and I struggled to see my float and even caught a couple of redfins by touch. Just where these super roach came from I don't know, for I could never catch them during the day. Contented, I packed up, hurriedly cycled home and went to bed.

I moved onto fisheries further afield to which I could also cycle, my favourite probably being the River Colne, where I had some good bags of roach, all caught on maggots in depths of no more than three feet.

My affair with the canal hadn't finished, however. Some three years later it was my summer holiday. I was due to start a college course in several weeks but there was no chance of a holiday. There were geology and zoology books to buy, grub and ale to pay for, and new fishing tackle to buy. I simply had to get a six-week job.

I found work at Glaxo Laboratories not far from home, and as it happened, the canal passed through the plant. Some lunchtimes I watched a group of workmen fishing the canal, and a few roach were being caught. I had to have a go myself, so one day I strapped a float rod to my bicycle and added a few items of tackle to my saddle bag.

Lunchtime found me on the canal bank a few yards away from the other piscators. There were no trees or foliage here, just concrete and stonework. The only greenery in sight was the workmen's overalls and the lettuce in my sandwiches – but there were fish waiting to be caught!

The tackle was simple; a rod and reel loaded with a fine line, a small porcupine quill, a couple of shot and a size 14 hook. The only bait I had was a few slices of bread. One roach graced my efforts during the hour's break, but what a roach, maybe 1½ lb in weight, a fish that my idol Mr Crabtree would have been joyful to catch and the biggest my fellow anglers had seen caught there. That was the last time I fished the canal.

Today I am fishing the Hampshire Avon, it's midwinter, and again the target is roach. The fishery is very familiar to me, for I have fished it many times over the years, mostly for barbel. It has limited access and I am lucky to have permission for what is an excellent venue. From autumn onwards I alternate between my two favourite species depending on what mood I am in. Today I am in roach mode, as I have been for a few weeks. Big roach are present in the area, for I had witnessed one biggie caught and espied a shoal of impressive fish during the clear water conditions of autumn.

On arrival I find I have the fishery to myself. The river is neither clear nor low, just the opposite. It has been in flood for weeks, is hundreds of yards wide in places and now the level is the highest I've seen it. My usual swim is unreachable; not only is the bank two feet underwater, but the water is a raging torrent. Not all is lost, however, for I have in mind a slack-water area which I have been waiting to fish under exactly these conditions.

The bank is completely under water, perhaps almost a foot deep, but I can reach it. My folding chair is just high enough to support my rucksack and rod quiver above water. The tackle is assembled by the car, water is added to a bucket of stale bread and crumb, the landing net is conveniently placed, and I am ready to fish.

This swim is fantastic; the former slack is now transformed into two large adjoining eddies, which, at their meeting point, form a crease where the current works away from the margins in front of me. The crease joins the main flow half way across the river and circuits the eddy. The aim is to drop the float in front of me and let it work its way along the crease of the downstream eddy to my left.

The tackle isn't complicated. A thirteen-foot

carbon rod is matched with a Speedia centre-pin reel loaded with a two-and-a-half-pound breaking strain line. On the line there is a good-sized Avon crystal float set slightly over depth at eight feet, and AAA shot are bunched sixteen inches from a size 12 round bend hook. My partitioned bait apron holds a few medium-sized slices of white bread plus some weights and hooks should I need to re-tackle. The line strength may seem a little light, but it has never let me down when roach fishing – fish any heavier and the chances of a bite are drastically reduced.

The float with baited hook is lowered into the water in front of me and it sets off on course seeking a plump roach. After a couple of trots through the swim I adjust the float slightly to the desired depth and pinch a small shot below it to hold it in place. It soon becomes clear that I need to keep the float on the outside of the crease, otherwise it drifts into the slack of the eddy and stays put. Also the line of the crease is mostly free of weed, but the eddy is thick with the rotting stems of reeds.

Every couple of trots I drop a kiwi-fruit-sized handful of groundbait in front of me hoping it will track the course of the float. Noticeably the water is more coloured than I've ever seen it. It's the colour of sand, and when I put my hand into the water I can't see it. Perhaps it's an unfavourable water colour, but the weather is fine, there's no wind and it is dry... I feel optimistic, and joyful to be here.

The trot I would estimate to be approaching thirty yards long, and I anticipate bites are most likely to come half distance. I'm proved wrong by the float "bumping" and going under at the tail of the swim. I strike and I'm into a fish, a good one. I bring it to the net and it is a fine roach, a pound and a half perhaps, immaculate in condition, fintastic! It is followed by another of similar size after an interval, then another, then another. All are from the same spot, and each is of similar size. They are unhooked

and quickly returned to the margins in front of me. The day is becoming a very enjoyable one, with some good fish, and it's great to be by the river.

The solitude is broken by what I think is a small bird behind me on one of the tufts of grass just breaking the surface of the water, but no, it looks like a mole having a wrestling match with a large worm. I'm captivated by its antics. After finishing its feast the furry creature paddles past my waders and has no trouble swimming across the turbulent river to the far bank. I decide to call this the Mole Swim.

Back to the fishing, and I lower the float in again and feed some groundbait in accompaniment. The depth in front of me is about a foot shallower than the rest of the crease of the eddy and it takes a minute or so for the current of the upstream eddy and enforced twitches of the float to send the rig on its way. This time though, the bait doesn't even reach the bottom before the float fizzes off horizontally upstream only inches from the reeds. I'm quick to react and strike instantly.

A fish is on, a chub probably, but unlike a chub it soon moves away from the edge to mid-river. A dogged fight follows and after a couple of minutes I ease the fish over the rim of the waiting landing net – another roach. This redfin is immaculate, plump with metallic blue flanks, and it is huge. I guess its weight – three pounds possibly? I quickly grab the weighing net and scales and camera equipment. The roach weighs two pounds, fifteen and a quarter ounces, a fraction short of a 'three', but I couldn't be more pleased, and it matters not a jot that it is not an ounce more. A quick photo is taken and the prize redfin is safely returned to the water.

Swim. Again the weather is fine, and yet again I have the fishery to myself, but the river is subtly different; the level has dropped an inch or two and the water is no longer a sandy colour but more like cold tea. More favourable perhaps – we shall see.

I put my hand in the water as I often do to feel the temperature. It feels okay but I can clearly see all my fingers, so the river is beginning to regain its clarity. I begin fishing just as previously; the float meanders around the crease as before, but no bite, nor on the next trot or on the one after.

I carry on fishing and catch a few more roach at the tail of the eddy, again all about a pound and half in weight. Dusk ends my day's fishing and it is time to head home. I feel like a pint, but the joy of the day is intoxicating enough.

It is now the next day and I'm back in the Mole

Two hours pass and I remain biteless. I sense the fish have had their feeding spree and have now switched off. That's roach fishing.

There's no mole to distract me this time but the arrival of another roacher does. It is none other than the ubiquitous Sylvester. Sylvester has a reputation for hogging hotspots and jumping into swims where others have recently caught, but I've always got on well with him and after exchanging pleasantries I tell him about my success in the swim. He tells me of a thirty-pound carp he has recently caught and where from. I know of the carp, for I have seen it several times in the margins in the same spot, but not where Sylvester says he caught it. I have no doubt it was thirty pounds. It was a mirror and as fat as a pig, but seemingly unattractive and possibly even suffering from dropsy and vulnerable. I have no interest in catching it; a big roach would have been my preference.

Sylvester begins to fish fifty yards away upstream on a higher bank. Still biteless, I decide to move. A swim further along the bank has produced one or two roach in the past up to two pounds for me and it might be worth a try. Today it is fishable, but the water is boiling, more so than previously. Even so I decide to have a go.

I can't help noticing that Sylvester has moved into the Mole Swim – how surprising! I fish on until dusk without a single bite, as does my companion. We both pack up and wade back through the flooded water to our cars. A blank day, but I'm still smiling!

* * * * *

Annual family holidays in my childhood were spent around the south coast, and one year Bournemouth was the chosen resort. The weather always seemed to be warm and sunny; I loved spending ages in the sea, despite the inevitable shivering and chattering teeth.

One day I asked my father if we could visit the nearby famous Royalty Fishery in Christchurch. My father was an occasional, fine-weather angler and was happy to go to this barbel mecca. I recall walking the riverbanks and noticing how fast the current was, and I vividly remember an angler

The Royalty Boathouse

13

ledgering above the Boathouse swim, using Edam cheese for bait. We focused on him for a few minutes and he was soon into a fish, a good one, which seemed immovable. It was unbelievable how a fish could put up so much resistance. It had to be a barbel, a fish I had often read about in Bernard Venables' books. The bronze battler was eventually landed and indeed it was a barbel, the first I'd seen. I thought what a magnificent, wondrous fish it was and resolved to catch one myself one day.

At the next opportunity I took my tackle with me to Christchurch, but the Royalty was full to the gills with anglers, so my father dropped me off at the nearby Winkton day ticket fishery. It was a delightful stretch of river, peaceful and picturesque, but no sign of barbel. I did catch a nice perch, which I was pleased with, and I do recall, with amusement, how a large rat came running along the bank and knocked itself out as it collided with my home-made wooden tackle box.

Not long after that, when I was about fifteen, I was gifted a holiday by myself in a B&B just a short walk from the Royalty. Not surprisingly I was somewhat naïve in my approach and tackle. The older, seasoned barbel anglers seemed to know exactly where to fish and were blessed with far superior rods and reels and copious amounts of bait.

There was an empty space on what was called 'Greenbanks' and I settled down with my float fishing tackle and maggot bait. It wasn't long before I hooked into a hard-fighting fish, which turned out to be my first sea trout. It was followed by another, then more, each one leaping out of the water and splashing about with fury, much to the displeasure

Ray Walton and John Medlow amicably contest a hot spot on the Royalty

of the fishless anglers nearby. Eventually I hooked something solid, and wondered why the river bed was starting to move. It was a fish; it had to be a barbel! It was a little scary playing such a defiant fish, but the overall feeling was of excitement.

After a few minutes I guided the whiskered fellow into the safety of the landing net. It weighed four pounds. It was well hooked, and so was I!

Let's fast-forward through the decades. I am now living within walking distance of the Winkton Fishery, it is a mild winter's day and I'm setting off in the hope of catching a barbel. The venue I have in mind is a few miles down the road and the journey shouldn't take long, but just a short distance down the road as I pass the Avon Village sign, I'm stopped by the local constabulary, who tell me I need to take a detour using the farm roads as there has been a serious accident around the next corner. The alternative roads are new to me; their barren hedges do little to conceal one ploughed field after another ready for next summer's crops and grazing.

The detour is through the western edge of the New Forest, but I'm only delayed by a few minutes. The ageing but trusty Volvo soon pulls into the fishery layby alongside two other vehicles. As I follow the riverbank at a leisurely pace, I notice the water is clear and a sizeable salmon that has been occupying the same lie for the last fortnight is still in residence. Two anglers are visible, one fifty yards downstream of my intended swim and the other perhaps twenty yards upstream, but fortunately he is just leaving and heading back towards the layby. So effectively I have my choice of swims with the other angler unsighted by bankside trees – magic!

Nearing my chosen swim, I unfold the chair and take off my rod sling and haversack, cautiously keeping low to arrive unobserved. Chair positioned, I can sit down and tackle up without standing. Rod rests are rehoused in the slots they occupied on my

previous visit and the right-hand rod casts out a cube of flavoured luncheon meat. The left-hand rod, aided by a jumbo bait dropper, feeds the swim with a cocktail of hempseed and other goodies.

A rig replaces the dropper; it looks incongruous, but there's method in my madness. I don't usually like short links, but now I have a fixed bead just five inches above a hair-rigged hook. Above the fixed bead is a double-holed sliding bead with a three-inch link of 4lb bs line covered in tubing, which ends with an American snap lock swivel holding a flattened ounce-plus Arlesey bomb. The bait is a home-made one. I found on previous visits barbel were picking up the bait, continuing upstream and dropping it; reeling in, I found the bait missing and the lead a couple of feet upstream of where it had been cast. On my last visit I drastically reduced the hook length and the strategy worked – I was rewarded with a fine ten pound five ounce barbel. If it worked before…

With both baits cast and landing net in place, I'm ready to enjoy the afternoon session. Before long the calmness is interrupted by a black creature bounding along the bank, and it brushes by my feet, oblivious of my presence. It's a big mink. I have seen many on different stretches of the Avon, but never at such close range.

With the whiskered carnivore gone, I can take in the broad scenery. The green, expansive flood plain of the valley is beautiful, fertile pastureland which leads to the darker tree-line of the higher ground. Boundary fences and ditches segregate individual fields, livestock have already vacated their pastures and the only activity is the sight of the farmer repairing one of his boundaries over a hundred yards away. A tranquil outlook perhaps, but very much a living one, with the fast water of the Avon like a live wire on a circuit board, every swirl, eddy, ripple or race on the surface beguiling the onlooker.

A couple of hours have passed and my two rod tips have remained motionless. Mr Farmer has left, and I wonder if any guests will arrive at my baited dining table served with tasty morsels. In the now fading light the rods are still visible, but I am now focused on the brightening isotopes attached to the rod tips. Any bite will be a now you see it, now you don't moment as one of the isotopes jerks into action, or it may be more tentative.

Minutes pass and there's a bite on the rod with my home-made bait. It's a subtle bump of little more than an inch, but it's just what I was anticipating – a fish has picked up the bait and moved the weight. Alert to the bite, I quickly lift the rod and I am into a fish, clearly a barbel.

The rod, an eleven-footer made of carbon-Kevlar, buckles over and I control the turning drum of the Allcocks Aerial with my thumb. The barbel, obviously a good one, plods around on the river bed in defiance, but I have full confidence in my tackle, which performs exquisitely. Using the strong flow of the current, the fish drops downstream and I follow it, grabbing the landing net in the process. Five minutes of unforgiving resistance pass and I begin to feel it is tiring and I am able to ease it towards the surface. She thrashes a couple of times on the surface and I gently ease her into the waiting net.

The weight of the fish in the net tells me it's big – very big. I quickly unhook it, fetch the scales and weigh my capture in a moistened sling. My estimation of the weight is confirmed when the needle of the scales continues past fourteen pounds.

Safely secured in the landing net placed in the shallow margins, the barbel is rested whilst the camera is readied. I seek out the other angler to see if he wishes to take the pictures, only to find he has gone. No matter – if anything I am pleased, for I always prefer to take my own pictures. The Nikon SLR with dedicated flash fixed on a bank stick and fired with a bulb-operated cable release performs brilliantly. I retrieve the barbel from the net and hold it steadily a few feet in front of the camera. An auto-focus red beam from the flash shines on my chest as if I'm in the sights of a sniper. Without moving I'm able to run off a few shots using my knee to operate the cable release. Pictures taken and the fish measured, I gaze at the barbel for a few seconds; I wish it could be longer, but I must return her without delay. Held in the slower current of the margins, the barbel soon regains her strength, and as I release her she swims powerfully off into the darkness of the Avon.

I fish on for another hour in the darkness, more in reflection than expectation, and then, with tackle dismantled I leave the swim. Euphoric, I load the car and Mr Volvo takes me home on autopilot, with no diversions.

SINNERS AND SAINTS

In a perfect world we should be able to visit a river or stillwater and find an abundance of the species suited to that water. Unfortunately, that is not often the case. Stillwaters fair better and often the fishing is good. The bigger specimens may well take a little longer to catch, but generally the angler will leave the fishery at the end of the day in a happy frame of mind. Many lakes and pits have been well stocked over the years; they may be commercial fisheries or club waters, but each has to compete for custom with the others. Those that offer poor fishing will soon be avoided, providing little income for the owner or loss of club membership.

Matches are popular on some stillwaters and the top guys will amass some considerable weights. Nets to over 350lb have been taken from a lake near my home. Carp predominate of course, but there are also tench, roach and perch. Surely there is no chance of barbel in a stillwater? In fact they may be there as well, as they are on many these days. Stillwater barbel are not my scene though, and I think the vast majority of dedicated barbel anglers would prefer to catch them from rivers.

The fishing on rivers can be harder going. Usually the density of fish stocks is lower but despite that, given the choice, I would prefer to fish a flowing water rather than a still one. It may be more challenging, but I find it more rewarding. Some river fisheries fair better than others – there are some outstanding waters throughout the country offering excellent fishing – but others can be rather

a struggle. It is not too often that we find a river looking like a Bernard Venables diagram with roach and dace in the faster current, bream in the slacks, pike lurking in their haunts, chub in their favourite areas and so on. River fishing probably requires a greater knowledge of watercraft, and the angler will need to be more adaptable, more persevering and more dedicated to whatever fish are sought.

Things go in cycles of course; some rivers may lose their form, only to pick up again after a few years. One river that is certainly currently on form as I write is the River Bann, in Northern Ireland. Press reports suggest that it is probably the best roach water in Britain at the present time; a 50lb net of redfins may not even get you in the frame in a match. That's some roach fishing!

On the whole things sound rosy, but that is not entirely the case, for there are constant threats to both our rivers and stillwaters. Let's call the source of these threats the 'sinners'.

One of the biggest 'sinners' has to be the human population of Britain, which is now one of the most highly-populated nations in the world. Mankind has a tremendous demand for water usage, yet the number of rivers is finite. Vast reservoirs have been built to supply the need for water, but an increased amount of treated water returns to our rivers downstream of towns and cities, and large amounts of water are abstracted from underground sources and rivers.

It is difficult to make comparisons with previous times; a hundred years ago we were in the period of the Great War, so let's go back to the mid nineteenth century. The monarch at the time was, of course, Queen Victoria, our second longest-serving sovereign, and we were still in the Industrial Revolution, which must have meant some pollution of our rivers, not to mention the untreated sewage that also found its way into our watercourses. Good fishing must have been had where the water was cleaner, but transport was very limited, except for the wealthy, so anglers had to be content to fish where they lived. Tackle was far inferior to that of our own time, but that applied less to the roach angler than the barbel angler. People were generally poorer compared to today and quality tackle must have been out of the reach of the majority. So the Victorian angler probably didn't have such a good time, but at least the population was not such a problem. At the time it was just 27 million, or well under half today's population. Urban development has spread vastly, and it continues to do so. Whatever your views of the current population increase, there is no mistaking the impact it has had on our environment and rivers.

My next sinner comes in the form of predators. Natural predators have always been about, but recently the populations of some have boomed. Cormorants are the first that spring to mind.

There are vast numbers of these black fish-eaters inland these days, and these voracious feeders have decimated many a fine fishery. I see them everywhere. On one small island in a pit I used to fish, I counted seventeen, and on one commercial fishery I visited, many of the carp had scars on their backs where they had survived attacks by cormorants. From the seashore I only see a few, but there are plainly too many of these winged rascals inland. The loss of many of the roach from the Avon and other rivers has been attributed to cormorants. They are protected, but can be shot by holders of government culling licences.

Mink have been very common too. Many were released by protestors from a mink farm in my area and they were very evident on the riverbank. How many have been caught by mink hunts since, I don't know.

Otters have been released in some areas, perhaps not always legally. They are lovely animals, but many fine fish have been lost to them, and not only in rivers – garden ponds have robbed of their koi and goldfish.

One practice that nowadays has just about come to an end is the killing of fish to be mounted in a glass case. Often, in bygone days, it was considered worth having a good fish stuffed and cased, if the captor could afford it. Thankfully photography has largely put an end to it, for almost everyone carries a camera nowadays and an image can be kept of a memorable fish. Moreover, it is morally considered unacceptable to kill coarse fish nowadays, whatever the size, and it is usually against fishery rules. It is generally illegal to move fish from one water to another, although it does happen, mainly for selfish motives. Fish stocks can easily be obtained legally and that is the only way to go. Illegal fish movement can carry a virus to another water, which poses a major problem to some fisheries. Fish stocks do represent a major investment for a fishery owner and a viral infection can have very significant financial implications.

I have kept the worst offenders, or sinners, to last, and they have to be those who carry out excessive weedcutting on rivers. I am not referring to the clearance of weed to create fishable swims or the clearance of channels to improve flow, but the total eradication of weed from one bank to the other. It is carried out on some waters and I would question of the farmed bankside meadows. Mechanical vessels eventually replaced the rowing boats and it was their efficacy and excessive use that led to so much damage. The newer generation of boats were wide, with fuel-powered engines, and could be operated by one man who lowered a scythe-like blade which cut the weed at riverbed level. As the blade cut the weed away, vast volumes of loose weed would drift downstream to be collected by booms laid across

The devastating weedcutter – the picture says it all

whether it needs to be carried out at all, with the exception of localised channel cutting.

Weedcutting on the Hampshire Avon was carried out for decades, with devastating results. Once, many years ago, it was done from a rowing boat with the weed cut with a scythe at the stern of the vessel; apparently during the last war, prisoners of war were enlisted for this work. The aim was to create a weed-free channel down the course of the river to increase flow and lower the water level to avoid the flooding the river at various points, which in turn would be removed by crane onto the bank and subsequently taken away.

The water authority's aim was to cut only channels which would have the desired effect of lowering the water level. In practice, that never happened. Often the weedbeds would be scalped from bank to bank. When the boat operatives were questioned about their duties, they apparently said they had received no instructions as to how to carry out the cutting. It doesn't take much imagination to understand the impact that such savagery had on the ecology of the river. Not only would fish fry be lost, but their protective and sustainable food source would be destroyed and mature fish would be killed or suffer physical damage. One angler told me that when a weedcutting vessel ploughed through his swim he saw several barbel rise to the surface, having sustained gashes, and they drifted off downstream, presumably dying. It was not only the immediate loss of fish – this was sheer vandalism and destruction of the environment.

Two other horror stories I can relate. The first occurred on a local millstream that was noted for its barbel fishing. One day two weedcutters came downstream, side by side, occupying the whole width of the stream and cutting everything in sight. Tons of weed accumulated on the surface, the water turned a dirty muddy colour and the level rose and began to spill over the banks. Young moorhen chicks, separated from their mothers, scampered in all directions. It was a scene of total devastation. As a consequence, fishing thereafter deteriorated, and catching a barbel became a rarity.

The second incident I witnessed occurred on a broad stretch of the Avon. I had been wandering the bank looking for fish, barbel and roach in particular. It was a short, unfished stretch and a pleasant one; beds of lilies, areas of ranunculus and clumps of reed mace all helped to fashion slack areas, clean gravel runs and shelter for all aquatic life. Then from upstream came the unmistakable chugging sound of a diesel-powered weedcutting vessel. The boat passed in front of me, cutting the weed, and proceeded to go downstream, only to return and go up and down the area from bank to bank. I took a few shots of the vessel (with a camera, not a weapon!) which I later used for an article in *Angler's Mail*

Good weed growth on the Avon these days, yet less sign of ranunculus showing the damage caused by weedcutting. It was a pity I didn't have a video camera at the time, for the scene the following day was horrific. I could see the whole, silt-covered river bed from bank to bank with not a single strand of weed or anything living in sight. The river looked like a scene from one of those American urban cop chases where the villain is chased down a concrete-sided, lifeless river with just a trickle of water –but this was the Hampshire Avon! It was heartbreaking to see just what had been done to the river.

Over the years, I complained endlessly to the water authority and highlighted the weedcutting problem at every opportunity in the press and urged others to do likewise. My complaining didn't always go down well, but that mattered not. Near my home there was a boom across the river to collect the masses of weed, which were extracted and piled high on the bankside. The piles were more than twice my height and I used to inspect them for signs of fish and invertebrate life. On one occasion I saw someone approaching me to see what I was doing – I don't think he liked having his photo taken and he ran off as fast as he could. The camera is often a useful weapon in recording evidence of any misadventure seen on the bankside – don't be afraid to use it.

Fortunately, some estates did not allow the weedcutters on their land, and they have carefully managed and maintained their watercourses in a sensible way.

I had probably gone as far as I could in highlighting the problems of weedcutting on the Avon and thankfully my good friend Ray Walton carried on the fight. Armed with his video camera, Ray was on the riverbank daily at dawn to capture the weedcutters' activities and compiled a film clearly showing the actions of the weedcutting machines, which was passed on to various parties. Weedcutting by motor vessel subsequently all but ceased on the Avon. Let's hope the practice never returns, and is not introduced on other rivers.

It has taken time for the weed growth on the Avon to return to what it should be and it is encouraging to see the improvement, although ranunculus appears to be less prevalent than before. It is also good to see the numbers of fish returning, but it will take time for the Avon to return to its former glory. Some areas that weren't ravaged by weed cutting have maintained good stocks and barbel to over sixteen pounds and roach over three pounds have been reported in recent seasons. Some fisheries have faired better than others.

So what is the lot of the modern-day angler? Apart from the population issue, it is not too bad. The barbel angler fairs better, for the species has increasingly spread throughout England and Wales, thanks to stocking in rivers that had no indigenous stock, notably the Severn and the Wye. They have increased in size as well, with big fish coming from many rivers. Tackle has improved greatly over recent decades, and these days lines are reliable and hooks strong. Roach are still abundant, but possibly not as plentiful as they should be on some rivers. Most stillwaters, excavated pits that is, are relatively new, and some provide good roach fishing. Indeed one has produced the biggest roach in history, and any further new record is also likely to come from one of these waters. Strong tackle is not so relevant for roach fishing, but modern lines are finer and more reliable, hooks are more dependable and today's lightweight rods can be comfortably held for the whole day.

Now for the saints. All in all, it is a good time to be a barbel or roach angler. Many anglers have been out on the bank, helping with working parties, meticulously looking after stiles, bridges and footpaths and creating endless new swims. Clubs and fishery owners have invested in stocking programmes, providing us with great fishing.

One of the many Environment Agency-reared barbel introduced into the Royalty at the end of the 1990s

Tremendous work has been done by the Environment Agency in looking after our waters in recent years, not to mention the many thousands of fry bred at their fish farm in Calverton, Nottinghamshire.

Credit also to the Barbel Society, which, in conjunction with the EA, has restocked the Dorset Stour with young barbel. Finally in my list of saints is the Avon Roach Project, which is doing great work in breeding redfins and restocking the Hampshire Avon with them. I am sure many other saints could be added to the list.

BARBEL - THE FISH

The barbel is a magnificent fish, strong in body and defiant in avoiding capture. Distinguished by two pairs of barbules, from which it gets its name, it is ideally formed to hug the river bed, where it has a tendency to feed and reside (though I have watched them feed mid-river and even on the surface). It is white underneath with golden bronze flanks darkening towards the top. The fins are often well-described as coral in colour, and they are thickly ribbed with strong rays, contributing to the immense strength of the fish.

The front pectoral and the twin belly pelvic fins are almost like rudimentary arms and legs. A few anglers have told me they've seen barbel ascending the sills of weir pools and even the main waterfall of a weir itself. I have not seen this myself, but I have witnessed hundreds of minnows working their way up weir sills with no trouble, and if they can, a barbel certainly can. If the barbel were an automobile, surely it would be a Land Rover Defender 110.

There is variation in the length to weight ratio; some specimens are sleeker and lighter in weight, others shorter and heavier, and the range of variation can differ from area to area. Fin sizes vary as well, and some barbel are identifiable by location due

A good pale winter fish caught in coloured water

to their fins. I find the larger-finned fish are more handsome and they often give a false impression of their weight, looking much heavier than they actually are. As with many fish, the biggest specimens are invariably female.

Colour can change with the clarity of water, with a tendency for the fish to be paler in coloured water, but it is only a tendency and some fish retain the same colour regardless.

Naturally barbel have teeth and a nasal system. Don't worry, they won't bite! The teeth are pharyngeal, in the throat if you like, and I am sure they make short work of most crustaceans. I once saw the 'cased' teeth of the 16lb 1oz Avon barbel; they were formidable bony structures. I have witnessed

smallish chub chomp up crayfish on the River Kennet, and barbel could doubtless do likewise. Tackling one of those giant North American signal crayfish might be a claw too far though.

The sense of smell has been described as not that great, but I am not so sure. One thing I have noticed is that with barbel on some fisheries, the hood adjacent to the nostril is much more pronounced. This hood, which I'm sure has a name to the biologists, presumably functions to increase the flow to the nasal cavity, perhaps suggesting that the fish are more reliant on smell in sourcing food, and further suggesting that the fish are more dependent on anglers' bait and groundbait. A fast-tracked evolutionary trait? Just a suggestion, but it won't

The one-eyed barbel

help you catch more fish. Certainly they are able to find a bait, even a black one, in coloured water in the dark without any difficulty, which dispels the belief that the sense of smell is poor. I can only conclude that barbel do have a good sense of smell.

My zoological studies, fishwise, have not been that extensive, ending with the anatomy of the dogfish, so my anatomical knowledge of the barbel doesn't go much further and any other comments would be by referral to publications, which I'm disinclined to do. Phylogenetically we are only concerned with one species of the Barbus genus in these islands, that being *Barbus barbus*. There are subspecies on the continent which can grow to a larger size. I have watched the movement of large barbel in Bavaria, unfortunately not in an area that was fishable.

I always like to have a quick but detailed look at each barbel before returning it to the river, more in admiration than anything, but I do look for anything unusual, be it just an identifiable mark, an abnormal scale pattern or any other anomaly. Fins can often have signs of wear, with visible chinks. The front ray of the dorsal fin can sometimes be stunted or broken. Some fins display a wrinkled front ray, most notably the anal fin. Scale patterns can be abnormal, especially where reformation occurred in early life. The four barbules show little difference, though occasionally there may be one (or more) subsidiary barbules growing from the principal.

The eyesight can show signs of deterioration, but I have never seen a blind barbel (a blind pike, yes!) The strangest barbel I have seen was a seven-pounder I caught many years ago. It was in absolutely pristine condition, fin perfect and beautifully marked, yet it only had one eye. The eyeless side had no eye socket and the head on that side was completely smooth. Very strange. I caught the same fellow again many,

A kinky barbel!

many years later and from the same swim. The eyeless side was the same, it weighed three ounces less and was beginning to show the signs of age, with the fins a bit tatty around the edges and the odd blemish here and there. Sounds like me, a bit careworn around the gills. Anno domini, no doubt.

Rarely barbel show signs of twisted vertebrae (scoliosis). One I caught, a well-known fish, was severely twisted but was otherwise in good health; it felt very strange in the dark though. All these quirky features add character to every fish and for sure l have never seen an ugly barbel. They are all exquisite.

Scale reading

A scale will reveal a number of concentric lines. These annual rings give a fair indication of age, though they are not 100 percent accurate. I did look at two or three scales from fish which revealed the same year class, a year in which the weather remained warm and sunny for much of the spring and summer, resulting in successful recruitment. I was never keen on removing scales, and discontinued the practice. It supposedly does not do the fish any harm, but it wouldn't do any good either.

On a fishery with a good stock of barbel, it would be healthy to see a variety of fish of different weights – three, six and nine pounders for example, with one or two biggies into double figures. If a fishery was known to hold only a handful of really big fish, that would be concerning. It may be famed for its reputation and doubtless give great pleasure to the few captors of the giants, but what happens when the weights of the biggies drop back and they fade into memory? In such cases the wise fishery owner or leaser will have foreseen the inevitable and considered a restocking programme.

The approach

Many articles will stress the significance of preparation in angling, which is wholly true. Okay, you cannot catch a fish from the comfort of your living room (though I know two or three lucky individuals living by the river who very nearly can), but there's not much point in driving fifty miles or more only to find you've left your boots in the garage or forgotten to take your bait out of the fridge. Successful angling is all about preparation, preparation and preparation.

Assuming you fish regularly, the first thing you need is a diary – two, in fact. One I keep as a factual record, and each entry is a record of a day's fishing. Details will include the date, the venue and possibly the swim, hours fished with start and finish times, the catch, detailing the number caught, and the weather. For any good fish caught the time of capture will be recorded, the weight (estimated in some cases with smaller fish) and the measurements (length and girth), if taken. The weather information will show the wind direction, water and ambient temperature (if taken) and a synopsis of the conditions.

What's the point? Well, we simply can't recall every trip. The memory does play tricks, especially with the passage of time, and a look back at the diary will be a valuable reminder of what and when we caught at certain times of the year. We all suffer blanks – it may be blank after blank after blank – and a look back at the diary may show that that was the norm for that month in the past. November, for example, used to be a very poor month for barbel; catches really took a dip, with the weather being

A first double is always much revered

Bert Careford, an Avon and Lea regular and a good friend, and a good barbel from the Royalty

particularly cold and dry and the water clear. In recent years the weather for that month has been much milder and I would expect the catch-rate to be much better.

My other diary is likewise ephemeral, but less so. It is also a calendar, showing when and where I have fished and caught, but there is more detail. Simply putting thoughts on paper will crystallise thoughts you have been playing around in your mind. Naturally I record successful days in more detail and dwell less on blank sessions, knowing what I did right or wrong may well be something trivial, but it will pay to remember it. It's all part of the learning curve. Blank days are not necessarily fruitless ones; many of my days are speculative ones, fishing new swims or areas, some days will be bite-less but I may well spot fish moving nearby or contemplate fishing a neglected area which may have all the ingredients of what could be a productive swim. Finding a good swim by your own efforts is much more rewarding than being told by others.

A blank day is never a wasted one; lessons learnt aside, it will be a day spent in a matchless environment. Don't go and you will probably regret it. My motto has always been: if you don't go fishing, you won't catch a fish!

In my diary I also keep a reel-related page. It lists all my reels, with the breaking strain of the line and the date it was replaced. Each time I go fishing I put another mark against the reel I used. I replace the line after 12-15 days of usage or a similar number of months, whichever is the earliest. I always buy line in bulk spools.

Fixed-spool reels may have four or more spools, and on these I write the breaking strain on the inside using white Humbrol enamel paint applied with a small straightened paper clip.

I always plan my season, writing in my diary what fisheries are available for the forthcoming season and short-listing my first, second and third choices for different periods of the year. I may refine the plan during the course of the season depending on how things pan out. I like to start the first week of the season after tench, but many a 16th June has seen me on the riverbank after barbel. It has to be remembered also, that in this part of the country there are restrictions as to what months you can and cannot fish, as game fishing and shooting seasons prevail. Thankfully the situation is less restrictive than in the past.

Often I will have fished just one venue intensively for barbel, just catching a few fish, albeit good ones, but I never fail to remember that fishing should be fun and deliberately take time out to diversify. Should I be denied a dabble for crucians on a picturesque pond or an afternoon for grayling on the River Frome in rolling Dorset countryside? I am still an insatiable fourteen-year-old at heart.

My final diary entry is a list of tackle required for a day's fishing, something like a list of what you need to take on a holiday. You may not need a passport, but don't forget your Environment Agency licence and club handbooks. Fishing several times a week hardly requires a referral to a list, but after a long break or at the start of the season, a look at a list will serve as a reminder as to what needs updating or attending to, as well as what needs to go in your tackle bag.

The digitally-minded may well like to take a different approach. Why not take a photo on each session with a smartphone or compact camera, which will record the date? Other details can be recorded the next day and each outing can be added to a file on a PC. Of course you may forget to take a picture, in which case just write the venue and date on a piece of paper, adding a sketch if you wish, and take a picture of that. A visual and descriptive account of the season can be viewed at a glance and printed off at yearly intervals if desired.

Any good tackle dealer will be willing to help you with all your tackle requirements, but I'd also advise getting one or two tackle catalogues. There are a few main mail order shops in the UK and they usually produce a catalogue free of charge – search 'fishing tackle catalogues' on the web. Sadly, like everything else, catalogues are becoming online only. I much prefer flitting through a brochure, and very old ones can be so evocative.

Tackle

What goes in the boot of the car for a day's barbel fishing? Various things would normally stay in the vehicle – binoculars, camera tripod, polarised glasses for fish spotting and eye protection, a few tins of spare sweetcorn and luncheon meat and some spare clothing. Not forgetting a towrope – I've lost count of the number of times the car has been stuck on muddy verges or slid into ditches and I've had to be towed out. I have a few chairs and my favourite, an early Fox one, would normally remain in the car.

I prefer the canvas hammock-style chairs with bars back and front. Chairs with feet may well be fine for landscaped stillwaters, but riverbanks are muddy places and feet simply sink into the ground. I cope with sloping banks by folding the rear bar under the seat. A thin, light cushion adds a little comfort. I believe Fox still make a chair with bars. My other chair is a treasured Efgeeco Adjusta, which is light in weight, waterproof and can be adjusted to suit any slope of bank. I use it for shorter sessions or where a long walk is involved. Clipped on the back of my rucksack, I hardly notice it is there. I've had offers to buy it – sorry, it is not for sale!

A rod quiver also usually stays permanently in the car, minus rods. Mine is a Wychwood, a brand I favour for luggage and clothing. In the quiver will remain rests, landing net and a lightweight brolly. I swap the brolly for a stouter one when the weather is inclement or the session is long-stay. For roving sessions, I leave the quiver in the car, just taking the landing net and a rod rest for use as a camera monopod.

The landing net is the brilliant 'Fastnet', a great bit of kit which closes one-handed with the arms folding back along the handle.

In place of rear rod rests I use a hard foam pole roost hacksawed down to a nine inch width; it has four U-shapes, ideal for rod handles. Screwed into a bank stick, it is perfect for one or two rods.

An unhooking mat is essential nowadays. Some fisheries won't let you on unless you've got one. Mine is a folding rectangular one which fits inside the folded chair.

Rods

Cane, glass fibre and carbon are all fine materials for a barbel rod, as long as the specification is right. One essential is that the rod rings should be of good quality, and lined. I have a preference for screw lock reel fittings – modern ones are light and provide total security.

Good split cane rods are beautiful. They are available from specialist rod makers such as Edward Barder, who make a Barbel Maximus, 1.5 test curve. Cane rods are a joy to use and feel 'active'. I still have a split cane Avon rod that I've had since I was nineteen, although I haven't used it for years, and at ten foot it's a little too short. It likes to come out of its bag now and then just to play.

Cane rods have two disadvantages though. Firstly they are pricey, because of the man hours involved in their construction, and secondly, in some cases, especially longer rods, they can be quite heavy. But buy one (or two) to suit your needs and they will be treasured for a lifetime.

Glass fibre rods serve a purpose. I used a Bruce & Walker one on the Kennet for a number of years as well as a three-piece Peter Stone Ledger rod on the Avon. Their demise came with the introduction of carbon rods, which are much lighter.

My favourite choice of material for rods is carbon or carbon/Kevlar. I started making my own with different test curves, but then while looking for an improved blank I discovered the North Western CC 125 rod, an eleven-foot rod with a pound and a quarter test curve. It performed brilliantly, perfect for roving for barbel yet usable for trotting on a small stream. Catching barbel to 12lb plus, I found the need for slightly more powerful rods, especially when static fishing, and I asked North Western to make me a pair of eleven-foot, pound-and-a-half test curve, carbon/Kevlars to my specification. They proved the perfect static rods, outstanding when playing big fish. The CC125 I broke (on a tree) and replaced it with an identical one but for the addition of a screw-lock reel fitting. I find eleven feet the ideal length for a barbel rod; some may use a twelve-footer thinking it gives better control, but in my opinion it doesn't.

The only other rod I've used for barbel in recent times is a Hexagraph Trotter, about eleven foot four with a detachable handle made by Bruce & Walker. I had it on loan – it was great fun roving for barbel and

I had fish to eleven and a half pounds using it. It was a pleasure to use and very versatile. Hexagraphs are, of course, carbon rods made in split cane style with a hexagonal section – I guess the clue is in the name! They make a range of rods, not cheap but less pricey than a split cane one.

I am a bit mystified by rods on the market today, the mass market ones. Many are quiver rods, as if that were the norm for a barbel rod; you may even get three or four tops. The quiver on a rod will have an optimum test curve relative to the dynamics of the rod blank, so if you get a set, just use the best one, the others will serve to prop up your garden plants. For barbel I find quiver tips totally unnecessary. A normal rod tip will register bites well enough. If you're expecting tentative bites, touch ledger and enjoy the scenery in the meantime. I do possess a pair of barbel quivers, it says so on the blanks; they are super-light and highly sensitive, and they are perfect for roach, but no good for barbel.

Many barbel rods are also twelve feet long with a 2lb test curve; necessary for whacking out a feeder on a big river, we are told. I've distance-fished using my eleven-footers on the Thames – that's a big enough river isn't it? – and my rods performed adequately. Shop around and you will find an eleven-foot rod with a test curve you are happy with. Test curves don't always reflect the power of a rod, as tapers and materials vary. Ideally the rod should be tested before purchase. The choice is yours.

One tip: Assemble your rod and draw a fine pencil line lengthways across the ferrule. Paint two small dots on the line either side of the joint using white enamel paint. Practice the dot size on a piece of card first. Allow 24 hours to dry. Future assembly then only takes a second, even in the dark.

Reels

Fishing tackle has always fascinated me, from the first sight of my father's rod in the garage with its centre-pin reel and float rig. There is something

The superb Ryobi ML2

about centre-pins; their simplicity and functionality make them so special. Early models are sought after and are highly collectible. Fixed-spool reels are also efficient and reasonably priced. They cast and retrieve line very well.

My first fixed-spool reels were Intrepids, which I soon abandoned once I could afford Mitchell 300s and the faster retrieve 400. I also invested in some Abu Cardinals. The Mitchells were good reels, well-designed and well-made and probably the best around at the time. They had problems though; the line was inclined to tangle around the drag setting on the spool and the bale arm could not be closed manually. The introduction of rear drag settings, skirted spools and manual closing bale arms inevitably lead to their demise. Mitchells did produce a new reel with these features and I did buy a couple but soon found there were superior makes around.

Finally I discovered Ryobi reels and bought the brilliant ML2s and the GR series. The ML2 was the perfect barbel reel: a smooth action, light and compact, deep spools and a matt carbon finish. Were I to replace them, I'd look for something compact, a

single, not double handle and black in colour, not one of those gaudy gold or silver flashy things. Not that I'm likely to wear out my fixed-spools, as I converted to centre-pins and predominately use them now in preference.

My early centre-pins were budget priced and poor in quality. The first decent reel I could afford was a Match Aerial, but I soon found it wasn't to my liking; the foot was too small, causing it to slip on the rod handle, the drum was too narrow and the diameter too big. I then bought a pair of Rapidex reels, which were good for barbel fishing. They were about the right diameter at four inches and I caught many barbel using them.

Wanting to extend my range of centre-pins, I visited the Hardy specialist and antique fishing tackle supremo Roger Still, who had an array of Allcock Aerials; I was like a kid in tuck shop. Had I the money I would have bought them all, but I settled for a minty 1920s three-and-a-half-inch Aerial and a late 1930s, maybe 1940, wide-drum Aerial, of the same diameter. The latter is my favourite reel. Not only did it catch my first big barbel but it is perfect for roving for barbel, being light in weight and great for

My favourite vintage 'pin for roving

The purposeful 3¾" Aerials for static fishing

casting off the spool. Later I added to my collection a pair of 1950s three-and-three-quarter-inch Aerials from Roger, which I use for static fishing. I've got a couple of other pins, a Ray Walton Rolling Pin, which I would also use when rolling a bait, and one for roach fishing.

I find four inches is the maximum diameter for a centre-pin. Anything larger achieves nothing and if they are too narrow-drummed, tangles can result around the foot. I also prefer to have the line coming off the bottom of the spool, which enables touch ledgering. That's my choice – others may disagree.

Many new centre-pins are available nowadays of various diameters. Some of the best are made by specialist reel makers such as Edward Barder, who make a four-inch centre-pin, Chris Lythe, who makes a four inch 'Barbel Master', J.W. Youngs, who make the 'Rolling Pin' amongst others, the Mill Tackle Company and Richard Carter, to name just a few. Discontinued and antique reels are also available from dealers.

I have the same regard for line guards as I do for quivers for barbel – these Mephistophelian articles are best thrown in the bin. They serve no purpose.

Casting

Casting from a centre-pin is no problem. Forget the Wallis cast, it is problematic and inefficient. In his description of the cast, F.W.K. Wallis called his cast the Nottingham cast and claimed a float could easily be cast over 100 feet – over-optimistic, I feel. That's a reasonable cast using a modern carbon rod, fixed-spool reel and a waggler or stick float. At least I agree with him on reel size, three and a half to four inches diameter, and the dis-regard for a line guard. Moreover, weren't the lines of his day heavily dressed and prone to sticking to the spool?

The Wallis cast necessitates the absence of bankside vegetation around you; a sideways swing of the rod is combined with a spin of the spool using an extended left arm (assuming you are right-handed), following through with the left arm as the float is projected and stopping the spinning spool with the small finger of the right hand. The hand on the reel is held in front of the reel. It's fine if you have perfected the cast, it's artistic and no doubt pleasurable to execute, but it can be bettered and shown to be anachronistic.

The Ray Walton 'Rolling Pin' in fixed and casting positions

Try the Woods cast – my own choice. It is so easy to perform that you can cast sideways, underarm, in any overgrown swim and probably reach the far bank on a smaller river.

Firstly, load your centre-pin reasonably well, say up to an inch from the lip. To practise, attach your reel to the rod, use the drag or ratchet to avoid over spin of the spool and thread the line through the rings and tie an ounce weight to the end of the line (apologies to left handers for whom the opposite applies, but we will assume the angler is right handed). Hold the rod around the reel fitting(s) by the right hand with the thumb on the spool; the drag can now be loosened and the ratchet freed. Pull off line sideways from the spool with your left hand, releasing it under control by your right thumb on the spool; two feet of line should do to start with. Keep the line tight, with the thumb on the spool and the left hand level with the right, ie 90 degrees to the reel, firmly gripping the line with the fingers.

The next stage requires a degree of co-ordination. Swing the weight away from you with a gentle flick of the rod, at the same time taking your thumb off the spool and allowing the line to pass through a loop made by the fingers of your left hand as if it were a rod ring. Don't move your left arm. When the weight lands, put your thumb back on the spool and rewind using the middle finger of your right hand to feather the line to the right-hand side of the spool. This will help with your next cast. Don't try overdoing the first cast – twenty feet is okay. Keep practising; gaining a few inches each time is fine. Resist the temptation to move the left hand forward – keep it still. With each cast you will have more line to the right side of the spool, aiding the distance cast. Gaining confidence and co-ordination, you can put more effort into the action of the rod and increase the distance between the hands to three feet, say. That is my cast.

"It won't work, it'll twist the line," someone said to me years ago. It does work and the line does not twist. I've used this cast for over twenty-five years and it works to perfection. A wet hand or fingers greasy from luncheon meat may hinder the cast, so keep your left hand dry.

Not entirely happy with my cast? Invest in a Ray Walton 'Rolling Pin'. The reel turns 90 degrees for casting with a twist of the spool, you can reach the far bank and beyond if you wish.

Fixed-spool vs. centre-pin reels

For me it has to be the centre-pin. I'll concede that the fixed-spool is superior in terms of casting, but I fish at close range most of the time and cope with casting a pin well enough whilst roving, but the unrivalled control the centre-pin offers, makes it the winner. There's more to angling then just catching fish, it is also about the pleasure and the thrill of playing a fish, hopefully a good one on the right tackle. A peerless rod and reel are a joy to use. Controlling a centre-pin by your thumb on the rim and regaining line foot by foot with the handle is magical in itself.

That brings me to:

Lines

When I started fishing, monofilament was generally inferior and the range was limited. Platil was one of the market leaders; it was fairly reliable but the diameter was high in relation to the breaking strain, from what I can remember. Some other makes were rubbish, their lines having fine hairs coming off the main filament. Hardly 'mono'! Along came Platil Strong, a thin pre-stretched line. I think 9lb breaking strain was the equivalent of about 6lb normal diameter line. Great, I thought, I can up my breaking strain. I remember catching a barbel of about 7lb on Strong without trouble, super, I thought. I hooked another about the same size and the line parted. I was horrified – I hate losing a fish. Obviously the lack of stretch was a problem and other anglers encountered the same problem. I think Platil was made in Germany, and strong it wasn't.

I tried other lines and eventually I came across Maxima Chameleon, which was terrific, reliable and lasted session after session. Talking to my fellow barbel anglers, I found they had come to the same conclusion. I was permanently hooked on Maxima (also made in Germany) as were the fish that picked up my bait. I have never felt the need to stop using Maxima for barbel, it has proved totally reliable. It's still available nowadays.

Today there are many good lines available: Fox, Korda, Nash and Gold Label amongst others. All market lines of 8lb breaking strain. Also sinking braids and fluorocarbons are becoming popular. Main line braids are very thin and supposedly more abrasion resistant. They come at a price though; 1000 meters is likely to cost over £100. I have never fancied using neither them, nor fluorocarbons. I am quite happy with monofilament.

Lines and hooks are unquestionably the two most important items of tackle. As we see on TV angling programmes from around the world, in some cultures that's all that is used (in addition to bait) to catch fish. It is essential we get both right.

Drennan Super Specialist Barbel hooks

Hooks

My experiences with hooks were similar to those with lines. Again I found the range limited and not to my liking. Richard Walker Carp Hooks and 'Goldstrikes' were both strong, but were a little long in the shank for barbel and once they lost their sharpness they couldn't be re-sharpened. 'Flash points' weren't a bad hook for maggots, but I began to find there were good and bad batches. One brand of hook I bought in a

Drennan Boilie hooks. A five-star barbel hook in sizes 4 to 10 - still available on eBay.

size 4, and found I could straighten them out using my fingers.

One of my favourite barbel swims on the Avon held some good fish. Fishing there one morning I hooked and lost a barbel and found the hook had straightened out. I switched to another brand and the same thing happened. Very frustrating. But at least I had a third brand to try; a well-known angler had written about it, extolling its virtues of sharpness and strength. I tied one on, a size 10, hooked a barbel, and lost it; once again the wretched hook had straightened out. I care to mention neither the writer nor the brand of hook.

But then along came Mr Drennan with his range of hooks. I bought some Drennan Super Specialist hooks in different sizes and found them fantastic, just what I'd been looking for in a hook. I've continued to use them ever since, as well as Drennan Boilie Hooks, and I've never had one straighten. Eternal thanks, Peter!

The Super Specialist hook is still available today, barbed or barbless, as well as the Boilie and the Super Specialist Barbel (which I have yet to fully test). Look no further than the Boilie hook for the perfect barbel hook.

Knots

Over the years I tried different knots when tying on a hook, tucked-in blood knots and so on, but as always I questioned what I read in print and experimented. I settled on the 'universal' or 'sliding loop' knot, which has never let me down. To tie it, put the end of your line through the eye of the hook from the side opposite the bend, leaving several inches free. Grip the line on the eye with your left thumb and forefinger. Make a loop with the free line using your right hand and grip the loop with your left fingers already on the hook eye. You should now have a loop gripped on the eye with your left hand. Now with your right hand, wind the loose end of the line back around the reel line and the side of the loop at the same time, making four turns. Add a little saliva to the turns, slowly tighten and trim off the loose end

with scissors, leaving a quarter inch (5mm) of end line. Dispose of any discarded line at home.

The Universal knot is the same as the Grinner knot,

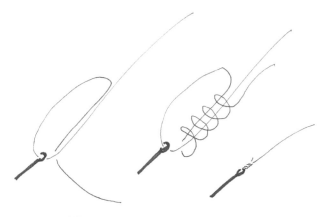

The Universal Knot

except that the Grinner passes the line twice through the hook eye to begin with. The Grinner is liable to slightly kink the line above the hook when tightening with monofilament and is no more reliable. I do not use braid, so I cannot recommend a knot for it.

Terminal Rigs

I like to keep my barbel rigs as simple as possible and only use two. Each has only one knot, the hook knot. I never have any joins in the line, no fixed swivels and never use any fixed weights.

For static fishing I use a link ledger stopped by a small bead. I like to use a small plastic bead of about 4mm. I still have some olive-green Gardner beads of that size, which are perfect. Before that I used to buy plastic beaded necklaces of the right size from street market traders selling jewellery. One necklace would last years. Korda make a 4mm rubber bead and Osprey do 5mm photochromic beads in different colours – I've yet to try either.

To fix the bead, I thread the line three times through it, overlapping the line, and tighten. The bead rarely slips – if it does, it suggests the weight

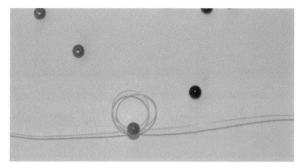

10lb line will easily pass through a 4mm bead

has been snagged. If it has slipped, I cut the line adjacent to the bead and it simply comes off. Any curled line can be trimmed off and the bead re-fixed and the hook re-tied. Four threads through the bead will totally secure it, but I prefer three to allow for any possible slippage through snags. Ten-pound mono will easily pass through a 4mm bead three or four times.

Above the fixed bead stop I use a sliding link ledger. These I have ready made up. I make them in batches at home, or they can sometimes be purchased. The sliding link consists of a twin-holed clear bead, to which is tied two inches of 4lb line, which is tied at the other end to an American snap lock swivel (sometimes just known as a snap lock). The snap lock is easily opened, allowing for easy attachment or exchange of weight. Thin, soft green silicon tubing covers the link line and knots, as well as the squeezed end of the snap lock swivel. A treble slip knot can be used to tie on the sliding bead and the swivel.

The small clear twin-holed beads are difficult to find. The only ones I've seen lately are larger in size and have swivels attached. Snap lock swivels are available, the smaller the size the better. Silicon tubing should be easy to obtain. The rig allows up to about five inches of movement of the line without the weight being felt.

I've changed my thinking on weight size when static fishing, whether with a baited hook or hair. I used to vary my weight from three eighths of an ounce up to just over one ounce (30gm) or more depending on the flow of the river. Just using the ounce plus (30gm) weight regardless of flow seemed to increase the number of bites; probably barbel

My standard ledger link

would be feeling the lighter weight and dropping the bait, but bolting when feeling something heavier. I'm happy with flattened Arleseys; flattened pear-shaped weights are okay but I'm not sure about gripper weights. They do what they say on the weight, but do they invite snagging on stony river beds?

I still do use lighter weights as a variation to the static method. Increasing the hook and bait size with luncheon meat in particular, I use a weight which is light enough to allow me to slowly trundle a bait through the outer, often weedier, margins of the baited swim. Obviously it involves using only one rod, and it often catches out an unsuspecting barbel. It becomes especially effective after dusk, particularly at the tail of the swim. The hook length would be twelve inches or slightly more. I may well use just one rod anyway, especially when I'm fairly confident of a bite, no doubt because I've seen fish earlier on in the swim. On smaller rivers such as the Kennet, I would only use one rod.

Otherwise, my standard set-up is two rods using the same rig with hairs baited with the same or different baits. The hook length would likely be five to eight inches on the upstream rod and about fifteen inches on the downstream.

I bait swims with a dropper using hemp, sometimes with corn, plus some samples of hookbait. My droppers have been made by myself or I've had the good fortune to be given one or two; they are big and hold a lot of bait. Some tackle shops supply large droppers, and Seymo make them in small, medium and large sizes.

On occasions I choose to bait up with just a few samples of bait, in which case I'll put several baits on the hook and up the line, cast out and strike once the lead has settled, hopefully leaving the freebies where I want them. Alternatively I may well use a stringer using PVA thread. Several bait samples will go on the thread with a small gap between each. The end one can be secured with a slip knot and the other end tied to the snap lock swivel of the lead link, effectively (in theory) leaving a line of bait on the river bed with your hookbait at the downstream end. Alternatively

Small, medium and large bait droppers

thread the baits on PVA tape, tie together the two ends and add to the snap lock swivel. PVA bags are not too successful in flowing water; they don't sink quickly enough, though stones can be added.

A stringer is always worth a try. Using a baiting needle, thread boilies or cubes of meat onto PVA tape and make knots below each bait and a loop at the top. With a snap lock swivel on the link the stringer can quickly be attached. The lowest downstream bait will be the one on your hook.

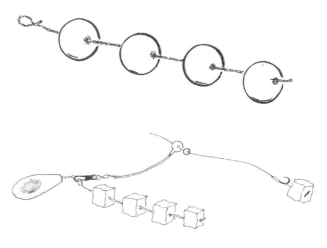

Returning to weights, I avoid using really heavy ones. Again it is about the pleasure of playing a fish. A heavy weight diminishes that pleasure, and for the same reason I have long since stopped using feeders, no matter how effective they may be. There's nothing worse than playing a fish and having a feeder flapping about on the line. Playing a fish should be a pleasurable experience, not prolonged, joyless or expeditious.

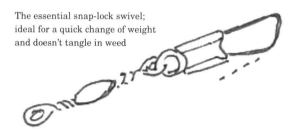

The essential snap-lock swivel; ideal for a quick change of weight and doesn't tangle in weed

Scales

I have always been fixated with weighing fish accurately and have written articles on the subject, for if I claim to have caught a fish of a certain weight, I like to be sure I'm spot on. I won't list all the dubious weighings I've witnessed on the riverbank, as there have been so many; "It weighs nine pounds eleven," says an angler weighing a barbel using a cheap spring balance. "Let's call it ten pounds," says his mate. Later in the pub it's a twelve. It happens.

To check my scales I bought a set of imperial weights from a company specialising in supplying weighing equipment. I've regularly retested my scales and those of many others. I used to do the odd bit of B&B accommodation and one guest told me he'd just bought some new scales. "They'll be wrong," I told him, looking at the make. Tested, they were several ounces out. He took them back to the shop the next day and bought a decent brand.

There's nothing wrong in the scales being an ounce out as long as you know it. They may, after

testing, be an ounce under at two pounds, spot on at ten pounds, and an ounce over at fifteen, for example. Simply write the discrepancies on a small piece of adhesive paper and stick it on the back of the scales. How do you test them? Buy or borrow a set of weights, or find a friendly shopkeeper with some scales you can test against. His won't be wrong, he'll face prosecution otherwise.

Don't buy cheap scales; they are worse than useless. Not only will they be inaccurate in the first place, they can read slightly differently each time you weigh the same fish, and may change with time. Invest in a good brand, but still check them. Digital scales are easier to read, but that provides no guarantee of accuracy, they still need to be checked. Keep your scales clean in a plastic box with a paper napkin covering the dial for protection.

One final point about weighing fish – avoid turning the zeroing wheel to its extremities. It can, on the tests I have done, lead to a distortion. Best to zero the scales and weigh the net separately, it's more accurate. Use the calculator on your mobile phone if you wish to record readings. It's all too easy to forget the simple things in the heat of the moment. An old net from a landing net makes a good weigh net, but will need dampening first.

Ruben Heaton are probably the market leader as I write; their Specimen Hunter Scales reads in one-

Still going strong – the accurate Avon scales

39

Aim to sit well back whenever possible

ounce divisions and goes to sixty pounds. The Match Scales are also good; they can be a little bulky though. Avon scales I have found to be good and are compact, and currently they can still be found on websites such as eBay or Gumtree.

Yes, I've gone on a bit about weighing your fish, but surely you want accuracy? I'd rather buy a Mr Bean-sized Christmas turkey from a butcher using a five-quid spring balance than find I've put a fish in print that is an ounce out due to my scales' inaccuracy.

Clothing

It is vitally important you get this right – feel too cold or get wet and you'd best go home. Waterproof gear is essential throughout the year; a summer's day with clear blue skies can change in minutes with the wind getting up and a heavy shower coming from nowhere. A brolly alone is not enough. You're on the riverbank and the car park may well be a long way off, so find room in your tackle bag for waterproofs, or wear them.

My preference is for a Wychwood jacket, which I carry throughout the year. If you're not wearing it

it's easy to roll it up and strap it to a rucksack. For summer I carry a thin pair of waterproof leggings which, if folded, can fit into the jacket pocket. In winter I like the jacket/bib and brace combo, bulking up with thermals and jumpers as the temperature dips. My bib and brace is also a waterproof Wychwood, though I prefer my old Rod Hutchinson quilted bib and brace, which is as warm as toast. A light scarf keeps the neck warm and I sometimes use a thermal snood, which can be used either as a scarf or hood.

In summer I wear a brimmed hat to keep the sun off and to aid fish spotting, and in winter I swap it for a none-too-smart barge cap – a force ten wind wouldn't blow me out of it.

A thin pair of Damart fingerless gloves keeps the hands warm. They are washable and though I've had them for most of my life, they show no signs of wear.

I've a wide range of footwear for different times of the year and conditions: thermal lined boots and thermal waders for the winter; wellies, boots and even an old pair of carpet slippers if there's room in my bag for dry summer days.

Not forgetting that all clothing should be green

in colour, olive green if possible. I'm not too keen on some camouflage wear, if anything it stands out. I once fished opposite three lads on the river. One wore a net face mask, and he was almost invisible amongst the reeds but for the fact I knew he was there. He was the only one of the three who caught a barbel. Put it this way, you won't see the armed forces in combat gear in the field, but they'll sure see you. The less conspicuous you are on the bank and the more you blend in with the surroundings, the greater the advantage.

If anything my rucksack, at 40 litres, is slightly oversized, but the spare space is sometimes useful when storing my coat on a warm day. It has three outside pockets, and the main front one keeps all my weighing gear, scales, weigh net, tape measure etc. The side pockets hold club books, glasses, a carp sack (which I have only used twice) and a torch. The main compartment houses camera equipment,

a compartmental Fox box (for hooks, weights, rigs, swivels, scissors, forceps, insect repellent, antiseptic, etc), pouched reels, bait droppers, a catapult, a small face flannel (olive green of course) for drying hands, bait containers and any food and drink I may take. I also have a small Fox shoulder bag with outside pockets which I sometimes use when solely roving. With the rucksack on my back and chair possibly strapped on and rod quiver on top of that, I'm hands-free ready to leap over any ditch or somersault a barbed wire fence (if only!)

Angling techniques – the pros and cons of fishing static and roving

Both the static and the roving approach to barbel fishing have their virtues, with few discernible disadvantages. The static angler will have the comfort of a cosy chair and feel totally relaxed. Most

A reward for the static angler - Trevor Smith's first barbel

Roving on a flooded river

of the time the rods will look after themselves, and a scream of the centre-pin will distract the angler from deep thought, incited by the fascination of the scenery on view. A large vacuum flask of tea or coffee and perhaps a savoury pie will enhance the pleasure, or in the case of my mate Trevor Smith, the pie will be replaced by a copious sandwich box and a chocolate bar or two. Trev is the quintessential static angler; a garden gnome would be more mobile on the bankside. That is not so say he doesn't concentrate – he'll happily touch-ledger for carp.

The relaxation will begin to fade as the sun starts to set and that magical hour of dusk arrives. With increased anticipation, greater concentration will be paid to the rod tips, but there may well be distractions. A ghostly barn owl may circuit the hedgerow on the far bank, two or three dabchicks may appear towards the far bank, then four or five, then ten or eleven can be counted; just where they

come from is a mystery. Fish show themselves on the surface. Ringlets will likely be a shoal of dace or even big roach, while chub will intercept morsels drifting downstream, their identity being broadcast by well-rounded dark fins and pale lips. With luck a barbel may roll like a porpoise, and the excitement intensifies ...

Roving is an equally fabulous way of fishing for barbel. You're in tune with the river – it has to be tried. Roving is a simple way of fishing for barbel; just one rod is required and much of the tackle can be left in the car or at home. Sure, a static style can involve moving between several swims, but let's assume we are talking about the angler who is mostly on the move and searching a stretch of river, predominantly with a moving bait. The rover may well cover a considerable distance, even retracing areas already covered. The method allows the angler to get a good idea of the configuration of the river bed. Aided by polarised glasses and reading the surface flow, the rover will have an MRI-like picture of the shallows and deeps, the location of weed beds and snags and the nature of the river bed, be it fine or coarse gravel or silt or mud.

The big advantage of this method is that it covers a great deal of water, so there is a greater chance a bait will encounter a fish. Some anglers will fish solely by this method, perfecting the degree of presentation and becoming very successful. The rover will likely forgo any form of seating, carrying a small shoulder bag, and possibly using a bait apron, with a landing net and a rod completing all that is needed. Though let's not forget the obligatory hooking mat, which could be rolled up and strapped to the shoulder bag.

The rover rig is simple: a baited hook and a weight a few inches above. Hair rigs can largely be forgotten, as they snag easily. Large non-toxic shots pinched on the line will suffice, or a light ledger could otherwise be used. When I fish this method myself, I pinch shot six inches from the hook or use a fixed bead, stopping a drilled non-toxic bullet six to eight inches from the hook. Most likely I'd use the latter method.

The style is simple yet requires concentration. The bait is cast upstream and allowed to trundle downstream, with a slight bow in the line. Your fingers or free hand can feel the line and detect every bump, stoppage and roll the weight transmits, until eventually the bait will swing towards the near bank and stop. Bites can be in the form of a gentle or a savage pull, and sometimes there can be a slight unexpected stoppage, and you strike and find you have a fish on. You may strike and wonder why you have done so, yet discover you are playing a fish; much comes down to experience. It may be one day all the bites come from when the bait is static in the margins. Where the river allows, you may be able to walk downstream at the same pace as the bait, in which case the bait will follow a straighter, more natural course. Don't forget your bag and net though, wear both if you can, or position them in advance towards the end of your 'walk'.

My preference is to hold the rod in front of the reel and firmly hold the line between my fingers, feeling for bites. I'm ambidextrous when fishing and swap the rod from arm to arm; after periods of time, it avoids arm ache.

My bait when roving will always be tinned meat. Spam is probably one of the best, bacon grill is also good and ready-flavoured tins of meat can be bought in tackle shops. I like to prepare the meat by cutting it into slices and breaking it up into rough shapes. I start with a couple of tins' worth in a plastic bag, to which I add a flavouring, be it spice, meat, fish or fruit based; strawberry is a favourite of mine. I shake the bag and keep it in a small apron along with forceps and a few hooks and weights. To bait a hook, I pass it through a corner of the meat, pull it through and slightly embed it in the greater part, leaving the hook point just exposed.

The roving angler will have an eventful day, because much, if not all, the fishery will be covered. Other anglers may be encountered and a good chat will follow. It's likely something will happen, and with luck it might be one or two or more fish, maybe just a missed pull or a chub, a pike or another species. The style can be likened to that of the salmon fisher of flies or the trout angler, willing the inanimate feel of the line into a burst of life. Will a big barbel pick up the luncheon meat? Will a hefty salmon be tempted by a Willie Gunn, or will a sizeable rainbow be fooled by a Pheasant Tail Nymph?

Roving all day may be tiring, but a damp landing net will suggest that it has been successful. Arriving home or back at the lodgings, the angler may likely have five minutes' rest, only to come to his senses to find that the clock has moved on by an hour. A hearty meal and a tipple will be most welcome.

Neither the static nor the roving style is superior; it's a matter of personal choice. For barbel I fish both, though I tend to favour static. I base my method solely on the density of barbel in the fishery I am visiting. Most of the places I fish have a number of barbel, some of them a good size, but much water can be almost devoid of fish, with concentrations in just a few areas.

On a prolific stretch, roving generally proves to be the best method. A moving bait will cover a great deal of river bed, inevitably encountering a number of fish. On a good day when the static angler catches say three barbel, the rover may double that number.

When the fishing becomes hard, catching a barbel can be difficult. Likely the river is low and clear and there have been sharp frosts on the preceding days. Most of the barbel will be uninterested in an angler's bait and quite often there will be just four or five fish on the fishery that will likely feed, maybe only one, and that is when the rover scores. The moving bait is the one that is likely to succeed.

On a fishery with fewer barbel, again the rover will cover much of the river bed and most likely catch one of those few fish – but it is not necessarily so, in my opinion. Much of the time will be spent wasted on large areas devoid of fish, while on reaching the barbel zones the bait will pass through in a few minutes and probably bypass the fish. A lot of the time barbel will just while away their time on the river bed. In winter the weed may have died off, but under the small remaining clumps, barbel will happily reside in their resting places, just wandering out at dusk in search of food. A rover may not even be in the zone at dusk. Also the course of the rover's bait is likely to follow the central line of the river, drifting at times into the margins. Often barbel don't favour the centre of the river; it is usually the shallowest part of the river, and in winter the fastest.

In the past, on hot summer days on the river, I've occasionally gone in for a swim when the fishing has been quiet. It's not something I'd do or recommend these days, but I did discover just how shallow the middle of the river could be; it was often silty too. The deepest part of the river was the margins; getting out of the deep end of a swimming pool would be easier than getting back onto the riverbank there.

Number 129 helps proves my point. What was number 129? A cow actually, which had the number 129 stapled to its ear. One day I was fishing a favourite barbel swim, and, as is often the case, a herd of cattle were grazing nearby. They were enjoying the lush green rushes and other vegetation of the riverbank, but number 129 stretched a little too far. She went udder over head straight into the river; the splash was enormous, sending a series of tsunami waves downstream. It wasn't long before the hapless animal was standing upright in the middle of the river, the water barely reaching the top of her legs.

Getting out of the river was a different matter; the water was much deeper at the edge and the bank was sloping. Not only that, every one of the herd in the meadow had witnessed the incident and cows, being the curious creatures they are, gathered at the water's edge, blocking the unfortunate 129's exit. She attempted to get out of the water several times, but on each occasion she fell back into the river. So there was this bovine bather in the middle of the river with her attentive audience looking on. Undefeated, she finally had the gumption to swim a hundred yards downstream to where the water shallowed and there was a cattle drink. There she was able to get back onto the bank, and her ordeal was over.

Getting back to the point, barbel, especially in winter, will favour the deeper water of the margins, even under the bank where it is undercut. That is not to say every river is the same, but in many cases barbel tend to be found close in when the river is high. It follows that the rover will miss much of the near bank areas where the barbel lie. Sure, a fish may be caught when the bait swings around into the edge, but with few fish around and often in a sheltered area, it has to be a static approach. Two or three swims can be fished using static baits, but my choice would be to stay in one swim. If I blank, I will consider why.

Margin fishing to me is just that, putting a bait as close to the edge as I can. If possible I will sit well back from the water's edge; the rod tips may not even reach the edge. One rod, probably the downstream one, will cast a bait a couple of feet out and I will bounce the weight as close as possible to the edge. The upstream rod may fish a bait two or three yards out over a baited area. That way any fish hooked can be played without the two lines meeting. The higher the river, the closer in I will fish. It has proved to be a very successful method for me.

Baits and presentation
Meat

Luncheon meat, as mentioned, is a useful bait and very successful – more than half my biggest fish

Watching barbel feeding is captivating. On one memorable summer session this fish drifted into my shallow swim in the margins several times, viewing my bait and ignoring it. Only when I whittled my luncheon meat down to a small sugar cube size did it finally take it. Magical!

have been caught on it. It is very convenient too, and spare tins can be left in reserve in the boot of the car. Spam is a favourite, and it's a good quality product. It was widely used in World War Two and carried by American soldiers. Spam – the name is said to derive from 'SPiced hAM' – is of course mostly pork, as are other luncheon meats. Most brands of luncheon meat or other products such as bacon grill will suffice as bait, though cheap, flavourless, rubbery meats that bounce off the wall are best avoided. My favourite luncheon meat has always been Ye Olde Oak, which I believe is still marketed. Although a little softer than I would like as a bait, it has a very spicy aroma and barbel love it. The only disadvantage is that it does come off the hook when distance casting, though a short length of uncooked spaghetti on the bend of the hook will help. To attach it, a piece a centimetre long is held against the hook bend while the bait is slid down onto it.

Another good meat is liver sausage. Again it is soft, but shop around for the sealed tube type and you can find a variety that is firm enough to use as a bait.

For hook-mounted meats I would use a size 6 Drennan Boilie hook; as previously described, pass the hook through part of the bait and pull the hook and line through the centre, then pull and twist the hook back into the bait, leaving the hook point exposed.

Fishing meat on a hair, I would use a smaller-sized bait. I slice up a tin of meat into sugar-cubed sized or slightly larger pieces, using the back of the knife to get rough edges, and put the cubes into a plastic bag before adding a flavour. Flavours similar to those used with roving baits are effective. One I have found very good with small baits is Nutrabaits' Sweet 'Cajouser'; the sweet/savoury combination of flavours somehow proves very attractive to barbel. The ready-flavoured tinned meat baits specially made for anglers simply need cutting into rough cube

shapes, or any shape you like. I've often wondered if cutting meat baits into the shape of a small fish fry might work; it would have a natural shape, though I have to admit I've yet to try it. Different hair rigs can be used – I will list them later. It should be remembered that tins (and glass bottles) are banned on some waters, so the contents of tinned meat need to be transferred to plastic containers in advance.

Maggots

Maggots are one of the most popular baits for barbel and account for many fish. Shoal fish are especially attracted to maggots and some big fish have been caught using them. Over the last century they have

The 'Fiddlers' area today

46

probably been the number one bait for barbel. But these days I never use maggots for barbel and haven't done so for a very long time. It goes back to the time when I reviewed my catches and mulled over the way forward. I had caught a lot of barbel, mostly from the Thames, Kennet and Hampshire Avon, in particular the Royalty and Severals Fisheries, yet had failed to land a ten pounder. I'd caught several 'nines' but just couldn't find a double. There was a misconception at that time that doubles were regularly caught, yet I had only ever seen one, a ten-pounder from the 'Fiddlers' area of the Royalty.

Big barbel, over ten pounds that is, were often reported in the angling press and I wondered what the secret behind the success was. Whilst still mainly using maggots, I analysed every press report over a period of time, noting the location, method and bait. At the end of my survey the results spoke for themselves; roughly 80 per cent of the doubles were caught on meat baits, particularly sausage meat, which was regularly used at the time, even though 80 per cent of barbel anglers were using maggots. So I ditched the wriggly things and solely used meat baits and sweetcorn.

I think it's the bait preference thing. Fish for roach, for example, with maggots and if you are having a good day you may catch fish after fish, the biggest maybe six ounces; switch to casters and you'll likely catch a larger stamp of fish, averaging half a pound say. Why the preference I'm not entirely sure. It cannot necessarily be bait size for a caster is no larger than a maggot. Perhaps larger fish are more choosey, leaving some baits for the smaller shoal fish and selecting the more tempting offerings which are irresistible. I'm inclined to think much the same applies to barbel; they do seem to be selective of bait, depending on their size. A generalisation only perhaps, for there is no doubting that big fish will succumb to maggots, especially if introduced in large quantities – just look at how they account for big carp – but nevertheless I do believe that if you want to catch bigger barbel you should pick another bait in preference to maggots.

Float fishing with maggots for barbel can be successful – catch one and you will probably get two or three. Use a sizeable float, well shotted towards the hook, which should be size 12 or 14; a Drennan 'Super Specialist' would be ideal. A steady stream of maggots will attract fish, a handful every cast or a bait dropper (small to medium) used frequently is necessary. Two or three maggots nicked on the hook works best. Catching fish of other species is a good sign, for their attraction to the maggots will in turn attract barbel. The more the smaller fish dart and flash, the more curious and impulsive the barbel will be. It is a style that requires concentration and you must be prepared to fish non-stop; have a break and you may well lose the shoal that you have attracted. It is also the most enjoyable form of catching barbel with maggots.

My old friend Mick was a great exponent of this method. His rhythmic feeding and trotting were mesmeric, and I seem to recall him catching 37 barbel in one day. A through-action rod of eleven to twelve feet with a test curve of one and quarter pounds or less is ideal. A lighter line is needed, as you won't get many bites using 8lb bs line. A 4 or 5lb line would be better if carefully used.

A ledgered bunch of maggots used alone won't result in many bites – this is where a feeder succeeds. There are many feeders on the market: flat-bed, finned, open end, window, caged, in-line etc. If I used a feeder, it would be one with a flip-end opening so it could easily be refilled one-handed.

Feeders are best used in conjunction with a feeder link; a running bead has a quick-change swivel attached. Drennan, amongst others, make these links. Fixed feeders can be used but are best

Ron Smith with a good barbel caught on trotted bread

avoided. Given the choice, I would ban any fixed ones. I've tested so-called safety rigs where the weight is supposed to break free, but it doesn't! Any breakage on the line is a death sentence to a hooked fish if you're using a fixed weight. Although I don't like feeders, I'm not against them, as long as they are free-running.

As with float fishing, only a small (but strong) hook is needed when using a feeder. Use as many maggots on the hook as you want, or a combo bait of maggots with casters or a small worm. Maggots can of course be used on a hair rig, a tactic that has been very successfully used for carp. Maggot links can be bought, or they can be threaded on a line with a needle and tied onto the hair. The wrigglers can even be superglued onto something at the end of the hair. Groundbait laced with maggots can be squeezed around the feeder to add even more bait.

Worms aren't used a great deal for barbel these days. The idea of baiting with thousands of them for several days before fishing, as was the practice on the River Thames in bygone days, has been consigned to history. Though I did know some guys who tried it on the Thames, baiting a swim days on end with hundreds and hundreds of worms, and boy did it work, they couldn't stop catching fish – chub after chub after chub! A wriggly lobworm, ledgered on a six or four hook, might work, especially in flood water.

Cheese is another bait that is little used these days for barbel, yet at one time it was regularly used along with maggots. Edam was the popular type used on the Royalty Fishery, as the consistency of the cheese made it ideal for mounting on a large hook. I'm sure if Edam was used again nowadays on a regular basis it would prove successful.

Sweetcorn was one of those baits that seemed to make an appearance almost overnight. Anyone on the 'scene' would have got wind of its success and it was soon widely used by barbel anglers. No doubt it had been used by a few in earlier times, and they must have discovered what a gem it was. Like luncheon meat, sweetcorn is a very convenient bait. Spare tins can always be kept in the boot of the car, and I recall visiting an Alpine tourist spot and seeing some huge trout in a small stream where fishing was banned. I fetched a tin of corn from the car and threw a few grains into the stream; the trout found them irresistible. There was a frenzy of feeding and soon I'd emptied the whole tin, with every grain taken. Quite an audience had built up, all gazing in bewilderment. Corn is that sort of bait; it can have instant success even when the fish have never seen it before.

Sweetcorn, of course, has to come from a tin, when it is very sweet and flavoursome. The frozen stuff is neither sweet nor tasty, and is less convenient. Some brands of tinned corn are better than others; I always look for the ones with large kernels, which aid better presentation. It is a case of shopping around to find the best brand. It must be remembered however that there may be a tin ban on the fishery, and the corn will need to be transferred to a plastic container in advance.

Sweetcorn is a dense bait and sinks quickly; it can sometimes be fed by hand, with a catapult or by using a dropper. It is easy to present on the hook or on a hair rig. On the hook I like to use three grains, sliding one grain over the hook knot onto the line with the other two grains covering the knot and the shank, leaving the hook point exposed. With a hair rig I again use three grains, threading them onto the hair with a small bristle already tied to the end. The bristle acts as a stop against the flat side of the last grain or fitted into the open end of the grain. In both cases I would use a size 8 or 10 hook.

Mix hempseed with sweetcorn in a bait bucket in a three-to-one ratio and you've got a great attractant mix. Again it can be fed into the swim by hand, 'pult or dropper. I would generally favour the latter. Some anglers like to bait several swims with the hemp/corn mix, then try each swim in turn. I prefer not to; I would rather bait just one swim and remain there. One or two barbel anglers I know bait swims on different fisheries on the two rivers in my area, flitting between the rivers and observing the response. That is what I call tenacious!

I have tried artificial corn and haven't found it as successful as the real thing, but I do like the look of artificial hemp, which appears very realistic. A few grains on a hair rig, fished over an area baited with hemp, is well worth a try. Barbel are highly attracted to hemp, sometimes feeding in a frenzy on it. Catch one and you'll likely find the digested stuff dripping from the vent. Hempseed is best bought in bulk; I've always obtained it from Haith's. They advise on how best to cook it on their website.

Bread is a bait that is well worth a try for barbel. I've seen double figure barbel caught by roach anglers float fishing with bread, and I had a habit of hooking barbel when fishing for chub on the middle beats of Throop Fishery, using small cubes of breadcrust.

Fish as a bait has often been written about, but I doubt if it has been tried very much. Barbel certainly eat fish, and many fish have been caught by salmon anglers using artificial minnows. I have caught barbel on the Hants Avon at the start of the season which have coughed up small fry, silvery fish, possibly roach or dace. The strangest thing I have witnessed again happened on the Avon. One spring day I was gazing into a deep weirpool aerated by the run-off of the winter's flood water. Minnows had no trouble in swimming through the deep, white

First fish to fall to a home-made bait

oxygenated water, and there were hundreds of them. All of a sudden a large barbel appeared from nowhere and swam through the shoal of minnows, gulping some of them down. How big the barbel was I wouldn't like to say, but it was big.

Are we underestimating the barbel's predatory instincts? And as I wrote at the beginning of this chapter, barbel don't always reside and feed on the river bed.

Boilies and pellets

We played around with boilies in the Wessex region of the Barbel Catchers' Club, but I guess we didn't fish them with enough conviction. It did inspire me later though to give a great deal of thought about boilies as bait, and I set about making my own. The subject of bait technology has always interested me,

but it is so complex; you read an article or chapter in a book without fully understanding it all, and by the time you have finished reading, you've forgotten most of the subject matter.

I decided to make a mix using just four ingredients, and the largest component I obtained from a local supplier. At first I got the mix wrong and the end product wasn't to my liking. I wrote down the ratio of ingredients, and each time I made a mix I tweaked the recipe. The final product seemed about right, and I couldn't believe the success it brought me with barbel. I also tried it for carp on a local lake and it proved equally effective.

Eventually I ran out of the main ingredient, as did my supplier, and had problems finding a similar product elsewhere. The alternatives weren't quite so good, but the bait did still catch. Fortunately you don't need a PhD in bait technology to make your own boilies (or pellets) for most of the work has been done for you by bait companies. You can buy products already made or make your own by buying the mixture and flavours in bulk, which works out cheaper, though it is time consuming. You do get a certain satisfaction though in making your own boilies and pellets, especially when you find they catch.

The bait market is now very big business and has gone global. Of course each manufacturer will claim their own baits are highly successful, and to a large extent they are. A manufacturer that makes a poor product won't remain in business for long. I would aim to choose a 'name' that been around for a number of years, as they will have perfected their product in that time.

Carp are not the only target market for boilies; barbel are not too far behind. Baits with a barbel label are becoming increasingly popular. The range of boilies and pellets is massive and can be confusing, and not only that, there are endless flavour enhancers, glugs, sprays and so on. For a boilie I would go for a small, fishmeal bait, but there again most are, though I'm sure other main bases will work on their day. I like irregular shapes and would cut a larger boilie down to the size and shape I want or cut them in half for a hookbait. I don't think it matters a huge amount which additional flavour(s) you use, it's something you can experiment with. One favourite flavour of mine is green-lipped mussel in powder form, which has a strong fishy smell. Open a tub, close your eyes and you'll think you are in Brixham Harbour.

With pellets, firstly don't forget not to buy floating ones or those which break down very quickly. Halibut pellets have been widely used for barbel and they are immensely successful. They are highly nutritional and it has been suggested that their usage has led to the increase in size of barbel in many rivers. That is likely the case, but other factors have to be taken into account, such as warmer winters and the spread of the species, but more on that later. Halibut pellets are now made by the majority of bait manufacturers and come in different sizes; they are best fished on a hair rig, either using a bait band or threaded onto the hair and secured by a small stop. Other pellets work as well, all are worth a try. Again pellets can be fed by hand, 'pult or dropper. One of my favourite suppliers is Hinders of Swindon, who produce a huge range of boilies and pellets, some baits being specially made for barbel. I have found the Elips pellets particularly good, which are now made for barbel, and you can now get Elips oil, as well as dumbbell baits in various sizes. Hinders used to issue a catalogue, though I'm not sure if it is still available. Their shop or website is well worth a visit.

The ever-popular Halibut pellets

That just about completes my bait list, but I'm sure other baits will catch. Sea baits such as mussels and cockles may work; they do for many other species. Think of a nice healthy English breakfast, bread, sausages, eggs (used for boilies) and bacon – they are all eaten by barbel. Why not try black pudding? Come to think of it I have, though from memory I don't think it sinks quickly enough. Didn't Fred J. Taylor once use chips for barbel?

Most baits are presentable on the hook, though hard boilies and pellets might be the exception. Some anglers choose only to use a bait on the hook, which is quite understandable. As long as the hook point is exposed, the method is fine.

When I first noticed hair rigs being used for barbel, I didn't think they would work. A 1lb bs line was tied to the bend of the hook and the hair length was anything up to three inches. Unsurprisingly, barbel were hooked and lost. Common sense prevailed; the hair strength was increased and shortened. I started to use the rig myself around that time and soon found how successful it could be. Sensibly the hair was then tied to the eye of the hook, tubing was added to the shank of the hook to hold the hair in place, and that about completed the rig, which hasn't changed for barbel over the years since. The only change has been to the hair end, and rigs can now be bought with all sorts of attachments to hold the bait in place; hair stops, screws, bayonets and coils etc. have all appeared on the market and I am sure there will be further developments in bait retention.

That does concern me a little, for I'd hate to think of one of these attachments coming off and being ingested by a barbel.

My own stops haven't changed since I started using them. They have either been a small loop at the end of the hair or a securely-tied bristle. If using a small loop I would thread the bait on the hair using a baiting needle and stop it with a small piece of dry spaghetti, from a handful I keep in my pocket. The bristles I use come from a plastic hand brush which I bought a long time ago; lengths of between a quarter inch (6mm) and a maximum of five eighths of an inch (15mm) are cut from the brush and securely tied on to a hair. The smaller bristle would be used with

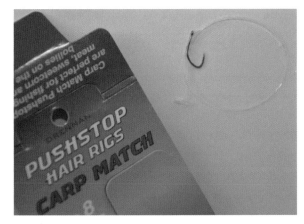

Ready-tied bristle rigs – although I prefer tying my own. The bristles can be cut off the ready-mades to make your own rigs

corn or similar sized bait and the hook, a size ten Drennan Boilie. Bigger baits would be used with a larger bristle with the same hook, but in a size eight. Fortunately I have never lost a hair rig or had a bristle come off.

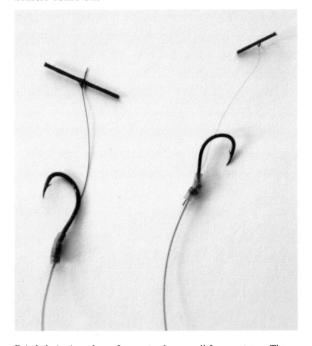

Bristle hair rigs – large for meat cubes, small for sweetcorn. The bristle length can be shortened on the bank using scissors to suit the bait size. The hair length can also be shortened by sliding the tubing along the hook shank and the hair pulled back to make a loop. The tubing can then be slid back to cover the loop and the knot.

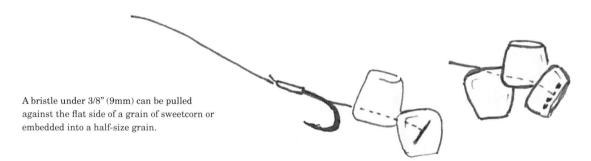

A bristle under 3/8" (9mm) can be pulled against the flat side of a grain of sweetcorn or embedded into a half-size grain.

To make a hair rig I use 4-5lb bs line, then tie on the loop or bristle. Six to eight inches (150-200mm) is enough line to make a hair rig. For a loop I use any small tubing or thin object (a large nail is ideal) and tie on a slip knot around it, tighten and tie on three more slip knots, tightening each time, then remove the tubing and trim the loose end. Use the same knot for tying on a bristle, making sure it is tight and doesn't slip. A tiny drop of glue can be added to the knot if desired.

Tie a simple slip knot on the bristle and repeat three more times, tightening firmly each time. The knot should not slide on the bristle. Adhesive can be added to the trimmed knot. Tie onto hook eye at required length.

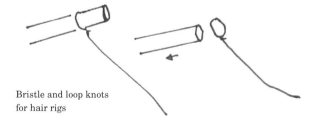

Bristle and loop knots for hair rigs

Tie on four slip knots onto something slender like tubing or a large nail. Slide off and tie onto hook eye.

Having completed the loop or tied on the bristle, I then tie the hair onto the hook. Tie the hair with a slip knot onto the hook eye, slightly longer than is needed. Pull on the end of the line and the hair will shorten; ideally there should be a small gap between the bend of the hook and what would be your imaginary bait. Once you're happy with the length of the hair, tie two or three more slip knots on the hook eye and trim off the unwanted end. Now move the knot around the eye, almost touching the shank, then with just over a quarter-inch (7mm) of slim tubing slide it onto some 8lb line. Slide the tubing a few inches up the line and then thread the end of the line through the eye of the hook with a couple of inches to spare. Thread the silicon tubing down the line, over the hook eye and onto the shank, and then pull the line free. The tubing should be fairly tight; trying to put it straight onto the hook without using the above method is more difficult.

It will now be easy to tie your hair-rigged hook onto your mainline on the riverbank, and the tubing can then be slid back over the hook eye to give a neat finish. Now you can thread your bait onto the hair, using a piece of spaghetti as a stop if you like (a packet of the stuff should last you about 15 years!), otherwise use one of the stops or pegs available from your tackle dealer. Bait bands for pellets can be tied on a hair in a similar way and there is a tool available to open the band and put it on the pellet. Ready-made hairs with loops or bait bands already tied can be purchased, and often they come with a hook length. I much prefer to make my own; I do a few at a time and keep them in a foam-lined container which goes in my Fox box. I've customised my Fox box by breaking some of the divisions using a pair of pliers; it now suits my small boxes and accessories conveniently.

Don't forget the remaining accessories: baiting needles (best take a couple), disgorger and forceps, scissors, a small knife and a sharpening stone. I also include a few sticking plasters and antiseptic in my box for first aid.

So you now have all your tackle and bait, made a final check of your list, loaded the car boot – it's time to go fishing. We'll assume I'm meeting an angler by the name of Alexander. Let's see what happens when we arrive at the riverbank.

LET'S GO FISHING

Alexander is a relative newcomer to barbel fishing and he wishes to widen his experience with some guidance on the bank with me, so he travels south to meet me. The venue is the Hampshire Avon and the date is the first of September; the fishery is leased by a local club, which Alexander has just joined. He knows the river by its fame and has read much about the Royalty Fishery and the middle reaches, noted for their history of producing great catches of roach, dace, chub and barbel.

His home is near Abingdon, in Oxfordshire. The River Thames is local, though as yet he has caught no barbel there, but he has spent three seasons on the River Kennet in pursuit of the whiskered fellows. He has caught a number of fish there and his quest is becoming addictive. His best barbel to date is seven pounds thirteen ounces and he feels it is time to broaden horizons and try another river, whilst still spending some time on the Kennet.

The Avon is about an hour and forty minutes' drive from home and he eagerly anticipates fishing the river for the first time. Although he has fished the broad River Thames, it was only near a weir pool. The smaller, more intimate Kennet is easy to read. He lacks confidence on how to fish the formidable Avon, but don't worry, I'll be at the fishery to give some advice.

As I drive into the club car park a few minutes late, the time is ten minutes past one; I see an angler waiting by his car. It must be Alexander.

"Hi, you must be Alexander, I'm Colin, pleased to meet you." He greets me in return. "I see you're geared up ready to fish the river, but I'd lose that cap if I was you, I could see the gold writing on it before I reached the car park and if I can see it, be sure the fish can. I'll fetch a khaki hat from the car and bring my chair and a small bag."

We negotiate a stile onto the fishery and I suggest we stop and have a sit down while I give Alexander a description of the stretch and a little history of the Avon.

"This part of the river is on the flood plain. You can see how flat and wide the valley is and occasionally in times of heavy rainfall the whole of it can be under water except for one or two areas. The gradient of the river is mostly low, and between Ringwood and Christchurch it is only three to four feet per mile. I don't know if it's true, but a farmer near Fordingbridge told me that that part of the river has the highest gradient."

"I'm no great expert on the history of the Avon," I continue. "It has certainly been used for navigation

The historic Fordingbridge road bridge

for centuries in the past, and Salisbury was a busy port. In Charles II's time, 1664 I think, the Avon Navigation Act was passed in order for craft to travel as far upstream as Salisbury and most of the work was completed by the end of the 17th century. Ten navigation cuts were made on the river at places such as Sopley, Ringwood and Fordingbridge and the navigation channel can still be seen at Britford, below Salisbury. The river must have been very different in the past."

I continue with my vague history of the river, and then suggest we see how it's looking today. It is fast flowing and clear. Generally it is weedy, but at present the growth is sparser than it should be following the weed cutting a few years ago. Hopefully things are improving.

"Well Alex, this stretch of the Avon is a little over a mile and half in length. We are at the downstream end as you can see, and there are a dozen or more good barbel swims. The best barbel I have had from this stretch was about thirteen pounds, which is about par for most stretches of the river, though one or two fisheries have produced some bigger fish. There have been some good chub, quite a few over five pounds and one or two sixes, but I've not heard of a seven. There are a few shoals of roach and dace, but they are difficult to locate. The odd big roach has been caught, but I've yet to catch one of them from this stretch. With luck you might see a salmon leap or even hook one. Carp are also present but rarely seen.

Sopley Mill

"Luckily here, at the start of the fishery, we are at the downstream end, so we are less likely to be seen by fish as we head upstream along the bank. Bring your tackle, we'll walk the fishery. I'll carry your bait bucket. Here's your hat by the way – hang onto it whilst you're down here! We'll keep way back from the waters' edge as we walk the bank, and I'll point out the swims as we go along."

"This first section is actually quite good. There are some rushes and bushes to give cover, added to wide bankside weed which also shields the angler. I've had a few barbel here, mostly on corn. The only trouble is the close proximity of the busy A338, which can be noisy; it is worth a try for an evening session though when the traffic dies down."

We move on upstream.

"We've got a higher bank here. The flow is a little too fast because of the small island opposite which channels the flow. Anyway there's no chance of landing a fish with these bramble bushes. It's best fished from the far bank, especially in winter."

"What's the depth along here?" asks Alexander.

"In front of us it must be six or seven feet. Downstream on the first section we looked at it is five to six feet, though there is a deeper hole down by the boundary of eight feet."

Strolling upstream, it is evident that the river is wider and shallow for sixty to seventy yards, but neither of us comment as we recognise the uninteresting character of this section.

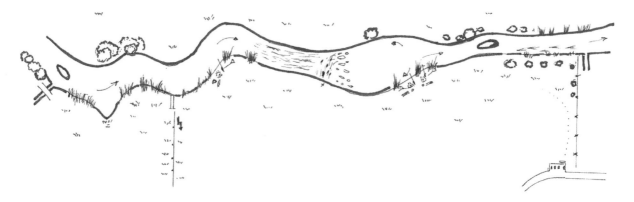

"This next bit is quite good," I tell Alexander. "The river is deeper, these high reed beds provide good cover and the two gaps are productive swims. I heard one of these swims produced a thirteen-pound fish last season. Pity they are both occupied today, but they usually are."

"Upstream there is a wider pool, but it's shallower and there's minimal bank cover. It's almost like a mini-weirpool because a shallow cobbled sill spans the river upstream. In bygone days it may have been a man-made crossing point."

The best spots are usually occupied

Alexander asks, "Is the pool worth a try?"

"No, not really, there are quite a few large boulders and it is easy to get snagged up. Above the sill is more interesting, there are some deep gravel runs between the bulrush beds. See those big chub lying in the slack water? Some of those are well over five pounds."

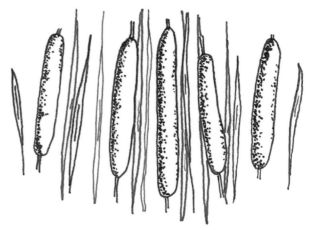

"The gravel runs most likely hold barbel, but this time of the year it's too difficult to get a bait to them. Winter is the best time to fish this spot; a good, deep slack forms in the edge, it's dead opposite that cottage you can see on that rise on the far bank. The river looks very different when its bank-high in winter, and any feature helps identify swims."

The next hundred yards is featureless – it averages just three feet deep and eel grass extends from bank to bank. We pass it by.

"The next section is good," I tell Alexander. "There's a deep S-bend and the river bed is clean gravel."

High reed beds grow along the first inside bend; we briefly stop to look at a good swim, one I have fished before. But we carry on. Around the next bend we stop and stand well back from the water's edge.

"This is a very good swim, there's a deep gravel hole surrounded by weed and barbel are usually in residence. If that chap wasn't fishing it, we would have given it a go. It always seems to be occupied, but there were only two cars in the car park so it's probable we've got the rest of the fishery to ourselves. There's another swim a little further along, but I try to avoid fishing near others."

As the river starts to bend again we encounter a fence, an electric one. I'm able to step over it, being tallish, but I suggest to Alexander, who's a little shorter, that he should open the fence using the insulated handle which hangs onto a hook. Undaunted, Alexander also tries to step over the fence but catches it.

"Ouch, I've been zapped! The blasted fence just touched my tackle," Alexander moans.

"Never mind," I try to reassure my companion, "We'll use the handle on the way back."

The next feature is the inside of a bend. The river is wider at this point and there is a large slack in front of us.

"Be careful of the boggy bank," I warn Alexander. "Oh – you've found it! Not to worry; the sun will soon dry off your feet and socks once we reach our swim. I think that swim is best avoided, although it looks promising, it's too shallow and silty and we can't get anywhere near the bank. It's only two fifteen. We've loads of time yet, you're down for three days aren't you?"

Alexander had already arranged bed and breakfast over the phone for two nights. "Yes, if that's okay Col, but I must give you something for the guidance," he replies.

"No, that's no problem, just pay for the fish and chips tonight," I answer. "I'll suggest a couple of stretches on the Avon and Stour for you to visit tomorrow; they're also club waters and well worth trying."

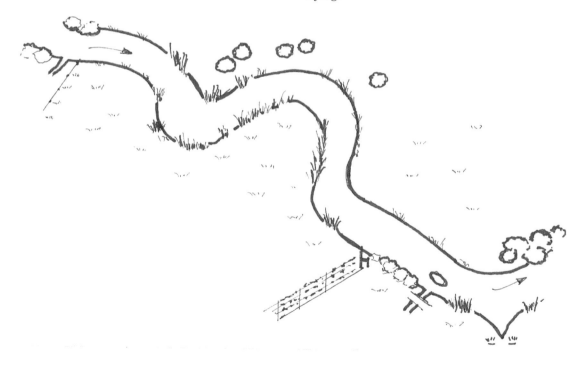

Wandering upstream, trees begin to line the bank and there are no gaps to fish from until we reach an open area, where a small side stream joins the main river and a planked bridge spans the ditch.

"This pool always looks interesting, Alex, it's fairly deep and crystal clear. I've caught good chub in the winter here but never a barbel. I haven't given up on it yet though. It looks the part."

The next straight is densely tree-lined and impenetrable. We then reach a barbed-wire fence.

"The farmer has just re-fenced this boundary with viciously tight barbed wire and the stile is too high at two feet with nothing to hold onto," I tell him. "Let's try and get through the fence."

I manage it and Alexander passes his rod bag, rucksack and chair over the top of the fence. "Oops, you've caught your jacket on the barbs. I'll free it for you. There's over half a mile left of the fishery, and no one seems to come this far upstream. There are four or five swims, some on the double bends you can see ahead, and the boundary swim. Beyond the boundary it's thickly wooded and the end swim is weedless. I've never seen any barbel there but it might be worth a try at dusk. The farmer once told me he saw a shoal of barbel in the area. At least you wouldn't get anyone fishing next to you."

As we head towards the first bend, I ask Alexander why he wants to try the Avon when his local Kennet is now producing such big barbel.

"There are barbel up to thirteen pounds on your local stretch, aren't there Alex?"

"Actually they have been reported to fourteen plus and the Kennet is a great river to fish. I have fished it now and again over the years and have concentrated on the barbel over the last two seasons with my mate Harrison, but I've wanted to try the Avon as well. There is so much history to the river, it's held the barbel record on two occasions as well as the pike record and there are all those stories of great catches of roach, dace and chub and so on in the past. The scenery is so different as well, the flood plain is so wide and the river has so much character."

"Right. Well, we've reached the swim I had in mind. There are high reeds all along the bend but there is a narrow gap, just wide enough for your two rods. Let's stop here twenty yards from the spot and see what tackle and bait you've got."

Alexander unpacks and assembles a pair of Avon rods, attaches Rapidex reels and tackles up with ledger tackle. The landing net has thirty-two-inch arms with an extending handle.

"Your tackle is fine, Alex. Where did you get the reels from? They look well-used."

"I got them second-hand from a website."

"Great. The rods are okay, but I suggest you try and get some matt varnish to take the shine off them; they make Fred Astaire's shoes look dull," I add.

Alexander scratches his head and chuckles.

Looking in the bait bucket, I see Alexander has brought some hemp, with bait boxes containing sweetcorn and luncheon meat, and he says there is a bag of pellets in the rucksack.

"I can't see the swim you are talking about Col, where do you mean?"

The reeds are mostly eight to ten feet high, but at one point there is a two-foot gap where they are only three feet tall. I point out the spot to Alexander and suggest where to put the unhooking mat and landing net, some distance downstream on the bank where the reeds peter out.

"It doesn't look like anyone has fished it. There are no signs of anybody having been here," says Alexander, observantly.

"Actually I've fished it seven times recently," I tell Alexander. "If you crouch down and quietly approach the swim with your tackle, put your rod rests in and place your chair on the left, well back from the edge, I'll put my chair over to the right," I whisper.

I join Alexander and suggest it's best to try sweetcorn on his left-hand rod.

"If you cast out just ten to twelve feet, I'll put your bait dropper on the other rod and bait up with hemp and corn. Sometimes when there's barbel in the swim, they immediately home in on the ground bait."

After baiting the swim with nearly a pint of bait I hand the rod to Alexander. "You could try meat on this rod, Alex. Try putting the bait a few yards downstream, closer to the bank."

I advise him not to talk, as any fish in the vicinity would be aware of the noise, and add that it's also best not to make any sudden movements. "Just point or mime anything you want to draw to my attention, Alex," I quietly say.

We settle in our chairs in the afternoon sun and Alexander takes off his boots and wet socks to dry out. Little happens in the next couple of hours; no bites, just the odd tap on the rod tip which has the luncheon meat offering. I point out a few buzzards purposefully circling above us in the almost cloudless sky; I mime 'buzzards' to Alexander, who looks up in fascination. Maybe I can get a photo of one, but my lens may not be long enough.

Minutes later another bird circuits above and Alexander points and mimes inquisitively 'buzzard?' I shake my head and mime 'seagull' with a smile.

The time is now getting on for five and still there have been no bites. Alexander has probably had enough of my company by now, so I circle around, keeping low with my shoulder bag, and whisper to Alexander that I'm just going for a wander upstream for a while.

There are two swims I want to look at, both in areas of reed beds, but with gaps to fish from. One swim is about eight to ten feet deep, but the darkened gravel river bed makes fish spotting difficult. I throw in half a dozen of my baits, which disappear from sight before they reach the bottom. I wait for a while to see if there are any signs of fish, but nothing appears. I move on to the next swim, which is seven to eight feet deep, and the gravelled bed is more golden in colour. I should be able to see any fish that are about. The few baits I threw in the swim three days earlier are no longer there; they could have been eaten by birds or anything, but for some reason only barbel seem to take the bait.

I throw in a few more baits, which quickly sink and are clearly visible on the gravel. Keeping still, I remain focused on the baits, at the same time absorbing the surroundings. A pair of deer bound across the meadow behind me and easily jump over the fence we encountered earlier. The unmistakable sharp call of a kingfisher can be heard, then moments later a turquoise flash passes by only inches above the water's surface, and although the camera is at the ready, I'm not quick enough to capture the moment. A heron emerges from nowhere on the far bank, wondering why its territory is being invaded. Still there is no sign of fish over my baits.

Then a large clump of ranunculus wavers in the current further out; could fish be lying under its cover? Yes, I can see a tail fin; it can only be one fish, a barbel!

As time passes, it makes no move, nor is it joined by others. My watch tells me it is now after six o'clock and I decide to return to Alexander to see how he is getting on.

As I circle round behind him, keeping as low as I can, I whisper "Any good Alex?"

Alexander almost jumps out of his chair in surprise. "Oh my gosh, you made me jump! No, I've had nothing, just those pulls on the luncheon meat," he replies. He reels in his tackle on the right-hand rod and the meat is missing. He casts in with the same bait and soon the rod tip is pulled round a few inches several times, then stops.

Barbel love sweetcorn in the summer months. Transfer a tinful into a clean plastic container before leaving home. Keep in the shade. Handy also if you're feeling peckish.

"Chub," I tell Alexander. "If you wind in you'll find the bait has gone. How they do it without being hooked I don't know, it's the same with corn."

Alexander recasts and the pulls begin again. Impatiently he strikes and a fish is on. He moves downstream, keeping his rod tip above the reeds, and the fish comes in easily to the waiting landing net. It's a chub.

"It looks big," says Alexander, "must be about five pounds."

"Probably is Alex, you can catch five or six of them around that size in a day. Pity really, for they don't fight on barbel gear and disturb the swim. Float fishing or ledgering on a cold winter's day they'd be great sport, but when you are after barbel, they can be a disturbance."

I take a photo of Alexander with the chub, which weighs five pounds six ounces. He safely returns the fish to the margins downstream. As we return to the swim, he asks, "Is it worth trying another bait? What about a pellet on a hair rig?"

"Yeah, you can try that, but I'd try a few more droppers of hemp and corn first."

I surreptitiously help myself to some coffee from Alexander's flask while he is baiting up, then return to my chair.

Seven o'clock, seven thirty and no more bites. The sun begins to sink before eight; I point it out and give the thumbs up to Alexander. The temperature is dropping and dampness descends upon the valley. Alexander has already put his dried socks and boots back on and feeling chilly, he puts his coat on as well.

Feeling peckish, I grab a container from my bag which holds some cooked chicken legs wrapped in silver foil. I snack on a couple and throw some wrapped in the foil to Alexander, who appears grateful. He seems a little curious though when he finds his flask almost empty!

The daylight is beginning to fade and I wonder if one of my baits might do the trick. I take a couple from my bag and circle round to Alexander, showing him how to present one on his left-hand rod. I return to my chair. Ten minutes later Alexander's left-hand rod slams over, the ratchet of the Rapidex screams with joy, Alexander grabs the rod and a fish is on. Alexander can't resist saying "What on earth is in that bait, Col?"

Again Alexander moves downstream towards the net, but this time it's no chub. It's a barbel. It plods around on the river bed, testing the rod to its limit, then heads towards mid-river, and Alexander has to let the reel yield line. The fight continues, and after five minutes, down by the waiting landing net, the barbel is still putting up strong resistance. Finally it begins to tire and after a couple more plunges it appears on the surface. Carefully it is guided towards the net, where it is gratefully engulfed in the mesh.

Alexander looks delighted. "It must be ten pounds, mustn't it Col?"

"Close," I reply. As I hold the landing net, allowing the barbel to recover, Alexander fetches his forceps, weighing gear and camera. On his return the immaculate barbel is lifted onto the mat, unhooked and put in a damp weigh net, and the needle of the scales starts to flicker around the ten-pound mark.

"Nine pounds twelve ounces," announces Alexander. I take a couple of photos and the barbel is returned carefully to the river.

"I had the same fish at nine-eleven about a month ago Alex," I admit. "I've also had a ten-thirteen from the swim but you've done well to get a good fish on your first trip, it took me seven sessions to get two fish."

We fish on for another twenty minutes and then I tell Alexander it's time to leave. We safely negotiate the insidious electric fence and pernicious high stile on the way back. Darkness has fallen by the time we reach the car park.

"Fishing again tomorrow, Alex?" I ask. "You could try having a look at some of the other waters on the Avon and the Dorset Stour, and then probably come back here in the afternoon."

"Yes, I think I'll do that," says Alexander.

"Good, I might pop over in the evening after work."

As I approach the fishery at five-thirty the following afternoon I see Alexander's car in the car park, so I park nearby, open the boot and grab my chair and bag and don my wellies. He's not far away, only fifty yards along the first straight and scratching his head again.

"How's it going mate?" I whisper as I sneak up behind him.

"Good grief!" he cries, spilling his coffee. "You made me jump again! Well, nothing so far, I've only been here an hour and a half, I'm using corn on the one rod. I had a look at another stretch of the Avon and after lunch I went to the Stour. Both stretches look really promising."

"You're in the right spot, it's where I've fished occasionally in the evenings," I remark, as I unfold my chair. "Got any coffee left?"

Over an hour passes by as sunset approaches, and again the valley is chilled by the evening air. The fading sun coincides with Alexander's first bite. The rod is almost wrenched from the rest and Alexander grabs it instantly. Four or five seconds pass and the line goes slack. Alexander reels in to find just one empty grain left on the hook.

"Could have been a barbel or chub, never mind,

63

The road bridge over the Avon at Ringwood, adjoining the Fish Inn

there is still over an hour left," I say, trying to reassure him. An hour passes without interruption, and a few minutes later I tell Alexander it's time to leave. Back at our cars we load our gear and he says he will treat me to a meal in one of the local pub. I gratefully agree.

Dining on a plate of sandwiches at the Fish Inn, we talk about the two days' fishing and I say to Alexander, "You've done well to catch a couple of good fish in the two sessions. The Avon is a splendid river, but the fishing is not easy. There are very good fish to be caught. Sometimes you may have an outstanding day, but expect more blanks than successful days."

"Yes, I've had a great time," replies Alexander. "I've caught my best barbel and that was also my best chub."

The next day, Alexander makes a flask full of coffee and buys some pies and fruit from a nearby corner shop.

"Many thanks for showing me how to fish the river, Col. I think I'll try that Stour swim you told me about, I'm looking forward to it."

"You're welcome. Glad you've enjoyed yourself. Good luck today and on your future trips to the Kennet and down here. Perhaps I might see you on the river again one day."

"Yes, hopefully, and here's your hat by the way. Cheers Colin."

"Bye," I answer, as Alexander gets into his car, scratching his head. In surprise I look at the hat and realise it's the one I used to carry a rescued hedgehog a few days earlier. Oops!

RIVERS

⟨————◦————⟩

This land of under 100,000 square miles abounds with glorious rivers, some famed for their salmon and trout, whilst others are noted for their coarse fishing. To my knowledge there are no barbel in Northern Ireland or Scotland, though no doubt I'll be disproved in the future.

In England and Wales, the two largest rivers are the Severn and the Thames, which are of similar length. These are followed by the Trent, Great Ouse and Wye, and all are famous for their great barbel fishing.

I have fished many rivers, from the south coast to over the border into Scotland, but there are many more I have not fished. Of those I have fished, not all have been for barbel; I have fished for them only in the Hampshire Avon, the Dorset Stour and the Thames and its tributaries. So I feel unqualified to write in detail about all the other great barbel rivers of this nation, although I hope my experiences on the southern rivers will, to some extent, apply elsewhere.

The Hampshire Avon

The Avon is my favourite barbel river. I caught my first, my most recent, my smallest, my largest and my most barbel from the river. It was once a two-hundred-mile round trip there from my Middlesex home and I made the long journey as often as I could, for holidays and sometimes for the day or occasionally just for the evening. Many holidays were spent in local accommodation: hotels, bed and breakfasts, inns, farm buildings, caravans, camping by the river

or on the back seat of the car when funds were low. Redundancy gave me the chance to move home, and the only option had to be a property within walking distance of the Avon. I managed to get a place which was seven minutes' walk from a barbel swim.

Barbel are not indigenous to the Avon. They first established themselves on the Royalty Fishery in the lower reaches of the river, having moved the relatively short distance from where they were originally stocked on the Dorset Stour. They thrived on the Royalty, becoming numerous and growing to record size. The Royalty became synonymous with barbel fishing on the Avon. The Great Weir on the Royalty accounted for a great number of fish, and many years ago some were furtively returned to the river above the weir. From there, there was no stopping them from travelling upstream. Between the Royalty and Ringwood Weir, there are no real obstacles; the sluice at Winkton top weir is often open and Sopley Millstream is passable by the main river. Even the now defunct Sopley Mill could probably be negotiated by barbel. There also seems to have been an introduction of barbel in the Ibsley area; whether it was covert or they simply negotiated their way that far upstream, I don't know.

Ibsley Bridge

Barbel are now spread throughout the Avon, but peter out around Salisbury, where they are few in number. Whether they are present in the tributaries of the Avon I've no idea. I've not heard of any coming from the Nadder or Wylye, though they could be present.

Despite the fame of the river, Christchurch and Salisbury are only twenty-five miles apart, and although the Avon might meander and divide in places, we are not talking about a great length of coarse fishing. Moreover, it has to be taken into account that parts of the river are in private hands, so no fishing is available, and there are syndicate waters.

It was recognised in the late 1960s and 70s that there was a noticeable decline in the state of the Hampshire Avon, which led to the Save the Avon campaign. Much of the decline was attributed to pollution, in part from the presence of large trout farms on the river, abstraction and of course weed

cutting was mentioned, but assurances were given that weed cutting would be done sympathetically. That never happened and on many parts of the river it became severe, totally destroying the habitat of the river, as I described earlier. Fortunately some landowners didn't allow the weed-cutting vessels on their stretches, and unsurprisingly the better fishing was on those untouched areas. A generalisation perhaps, but I have no doubt savage weed cutting led to the severe decline of the Avon. A glance through the weekly magazines over recent years will show few, if any, big barbel reported from the river.

It might sound as if I'm maligning the Avon, but far from it, I have great affection for the river and only wish it could return to its former glory. If everyone pulls together, improvements should be seen in the quality of the river's ecology and the recovery of fish stocks.

On some stretches where I have fished for years, the barbel fishing is not what it was. To give one example, some time ago I had two and half hours to spare one evening, and fishing a local stretch I had three good barbel, one a double, and a good chub. I'd have caught more, for they were still feeding, but I had to leave the fishery due to club rules. The last time I fished the stretch I had one barbel in a whole season and night fishing was available. On other stretches the barbel fishing is status quo, the population remains much the same as far as I am aware and in fact there are some bigger fish around.

barbel have been caught in recent times. It follows that these are no doubt re-captures of thirteen and fourteen-pound fish caught a few years ago; a sixteen pounder doesn't achieve that weight overnight.

The prophesy of a very big barbel was realised with a massive 19lb 11oz fish caught by Pete Reading in March 2019. Pete is a top angler, someone I greatly respect, and like me he has the Avon flowing through his veins. The fish looks awesome in the photo on the web – well done Pete.

Another barbel hooked in the margins

It is apparent there are fewer anglers on the bank. River fishing is never easy, especially for barbel, and it is not unusual to go home at the end of the day with a dry landing net. Perhaps one of the reasons is the pre-eminence of stillwater 'commercials' where the fishing is easy and it does seem that the river angler is more specialist for want of a better word. Those that I meet on the bank do seem to be more 'clued up'.

So the Avon is a difficult river and barbel fishing is hard going, but the chances of a very big barbel are probably greater than ever. As far as I know three different sixteens and a seventeen-pound-plus

The Royalty Fishery

This fishery always commands special attention. Before the middle reaches rose to fame It accounted for most of the barbel caught from the Hampshire Avon, and it still produces some very good fish. There may be fewer barbel nowadays, but catch one here and there is a good chance it will be over ten pounds. It is still a fishery where roving would be my choice of method. The Royalty is a unique fishery. It is like a microcosm of a whole river system with every conceivable type of swim you can imagine; there are

Gravelly runs on 'Greenbanks'

The famous Bridge Pool

many bends, deeps, shallows, weir pools, rapids, fast runs and slack areas.

Most of the swims, like the Compound, Parlour, Pipes, Greenbanks, Railway Pool, Fiddlers, the Boat House and the House Pool, will be familiar to many barbel anglers, and these are still amongst the most popular and productive swims. Few though try the lower stretch, and apart from the start and finish of the season I rarely see anyone fishing above and below the bypass (the A35). Admittedly it is not the most attractive part of the fishery because of the main road, but it is an area well worth a try and in the past barbel have been caught as far downstream as the Bridge Pool in the town centre.

The Royalty has been kind to me over many years, and more often than not I have caught barbel there, regardless of the conditions. Just thinking with eyes closed of one of my favourite swims, I can imagine that pull on the line that results in a hooked barbel. Dreamtastic!

Royalty barbel play by their own rules though. If you think you know all there is to know about barbel, you'll likely be dumbfounded by results. You may well catch a few decent-sized barbel over several days of intense fishing and then along comes a novice who catches a thirteen-pounder – it happens quite often. Barbel have been caught to over sixteen pounds recently and there is always a chance of a bigger fish. But best not think of a monster; relish in the history of the fishery, of all the famous anglers who have walked its banks, and be happy with whatever you catch, even if it is only a whisper of the spirit of bygone days.

Not a biggie, but a welcome gift on Christmas Day

Adjacent to the Royalty main car park, by the footbridge, the Rod Room can be found. This historic room, frequented by many famous anglers over the decades, is now the Royalty Fishery Museum. Tony Timms, a lifelong angler, is the curator. Tony has extensively researched the history of the Royalty and the Avon and has built up a tremendous array of angling memorabilia. One wall is adorned with some casts of huge salmon, the biggest a 49lb fish, beautifully painted by the gifted artist and angler John Searl. There is also a free-standing, realistic, facsimile barbel, which has the dimensions of a fish weighing upwards of sixteen pounds. A huge gallery of photographs of big fish and famous anglers from Richard Walker to Ray Walton grace at least one wall and there's even a picture of the great Wallis. There are also assembled rods and reels, old weighing scales, books and I couldn't help but notice out the corner of my eye on my last visit, a number of vintage floats, which had me drooling. A visit to the museum is worth the price of a day ticket alone.

The facsimile barbel

Tony Timms in the Royalty Fishery Museum

70

The Avon Valley Path runs from Christchurch to Salisbury and some of the Royalty can be seen from behind the fencing, but to enter the fishery a ticket has to be purchased in advance. Tickets are only available from Davis Tackle in Bargates, Christchurch. Night fishing, I believe, is still allowed on a limited basis and some club membership allows a limited number of tickets, which again have to be obtained in advance from Davis Tackle. Unhooking mats are required. I am not aware of any free fishing on the Hampshire Avon. Day tickets are available on some stretches in addition to the Royalty, Ringwood Tackle sells day tickets for local stretches, Fordingbridge Recreation Park sell day tickets which can be bought from the nearby kiosk, in the Downton area tickets can be bought for the Salisbury Angling Club water and currently day tickets are available for the London Angling Association water at Britford, where barbel to ten pounds have been reported. Permission can also be found on a few other stretches and tackle shops should be able to give further advice.

Some fishing is syndicated, and is worth the expense for the ardent angler. Local angling clubs are a good option, the main ones being Christchurch Angling Club, Ringwood & District AA and Salisbury and District AC. Local tackle shops should have details of membership, or application forms can be completed on line.

Some clubs have concessions to fish certain day ticket waters, and they have some of the prime barbel fishing on the nearby Dorset Stour.

The Dorset Stour

The Stour is less familiar to me than the Avon; I guess this stems from the time when I had to make the long journey to the Avon valley, and the Stour

Ringwood Weir in bygone days. The opposite bank is part of Ringwood Fishery, which extends below the town. Ringwood Tackle, 5 The Bridges, West Street BH24 1EA, sell day tickets and club membership books.

Ibsley - difficult but rewarding

was that bit further and did not justify yet more travelling time. The Avon has been enough to keep me interested, with big barbel on many stretches. Yet the Stour is equally famed for its big barbel and in fact has accounted for larger fish. I can think of three, maybe four fish over eighteen pounds, and one is rumoured to have been over nineteen. Of course they are only rumours, but that applies to many big fish caught throughout the country.

Despite my preference for the Avon, I have fished the Stour a fair number of times, from the tidal reach at Christchurch Quay to Throop Fishery and above to the Wimborne area. I've also done features for magazines on venues further upstream at places like Fiddleford, Sturminster Newton and fisheries in the Blackmoor Vale. I have caught a number of Stour barbel, mostly from Throop Fishery. I understand that as I write, Ringwood & District AA control the

lower Stour upstream to Throop Fishery, where the downstream boundary has been extended to Iford Bridge. The lower Stour offers outstanding fishing. Day tickets are available from local tackle shops.

The river varies in character throughout. It is tidal up to Iford Bridge and above, where mullet migrate to in the spring and early summer. I've seen many on the middle beats at Throop and caught one or two in the past. Throop Fishery is a long stretch, with something like five miles of bank fishing. There are weir pools, deep pools and gravel runs throughout with good weed growth. The barbel fishing is tremendous. There are three beats on Throop with different access points. Ringwood & District AA control the fishing and day tickets are available. The nearest tackle shops are Christchurch Angling Centre, Davis Tackle in Christchurch and Bournemouth Fishing Lodge. I must admit that on

The picturesque Dorset Stour at Ensbury Bridge

The inviting Stour at River Way recreation ground – now part of Throop beat 3

recent visits I've fished Throop for chub; there are some superb ones on the fishery. For barbel I would try two or three swims in a session, settling in the most likely spot before the sun sets. The fishery is well bailiffed and I would advise the visiting angler to seek their advice; the bailiffs are far more knowledgeable about barbel on the fishery than I am.

Above Throop much of the fishing is controlled

The free stretch on the Dorset Stour at Muscliff offers huge potential for big barbel and good roach

by Ringwood & DAA and Christchurch AC, and membership of these clubs is well worth considering. There are some huge barbel in the area between Throop and Wimborne, but they can be localised and the fishing can be hard going. The best bet is to try two or three areas and have a friendly chat with other anglers on the bank. If I was looking for a river record or just a biggie, I would concentrate on the area between Muscliff in north Bournemouth and the environs of Wimborne.

There are two good free fishing areas on the Stour, both on the south bank. Above Throop there is a long free stretch between Muscliff and below the properties at Ensbury Bridge. It is best accessed from the car park at the recreation ground in Granby Road, off Muscliffe Lane. A path leads from the car park to the river; from there I favour the downstream area, which is narrower and faster flowing, with abundant weed growth. The stretch extends down to the top boundary of Throop Fishery. You may have to compete with local anglers and picnickers, especially in the summer months, but barbel are present and there are some very good ones. Some of the swims above the entry point have been lost due to a recently-installed bankside walkway, and there is now a visitors' centre by the side of the path leading to the river, where, I believe, hot drinks are available. I've never seen so many dogs in one place as I have here, other than at a dog show, so keep all bait out of sight and leave no baited hooks lying on the bank. I would rate this Bournemouth Borough Council-controlled water very highly.

The other free stretch is below Longham Bridge on the right bank. Initially it is shallow but anywhere from where the high bank begins to the end of the fishery, where a stream joins the river, is well

The challenging free stretch at Longham

worth trying. It is not a long stretch but has always produced good barbel. There are reports of barbel to eighteen pounds, but how genuine they are I don't know. Parking is limited in the slip road by the bridge and take care when crossing the busy A348. There may be parking further south in the Millhams Road area and accessing the fishery via the Stour Valley Way, but I've yet to investigate. Again be prepared for bankside disturbances early season. However

I revisited the fishery very recently to take some pictures on a pleasant sunny day and was surprised how quiet it was; I only saw one angler, a roving float fisher, and a Bournemouth Council patrol vehicle. The riverbank fringes the northern side of Millham Meads Nature Reserve. One good swim has been lost to bankside erosion, but otherwise the stretch looks fantastic, most swims are mouth-watering and just spell barbel. Towards the bridge there were literally hundreds of roach, shoaled up below the weed beds – not big fish, but from the two or three-year-old class, which is very promising for the future. There was the odd sign of litter and the remains of bonfires, so please take home all your litter and don't light any fires. The fishery is truly delightful and offers huge potential, though the 'disagreeable element' has to be considered.

Wimborne & District Angling Club also have some good stretches of the Stour. Membership can be arranged on line. Barbel have been present in the Wimborne area, with fish over fourteen pounds.

I know little of the distribution of barbel above Wimborne. I have heard of fish being seen below Blandford, but that is the extent of my knowledge of barbel in the middle reaches of the Stour.

Above Blandford Forum there are some truly delightful sections of the Stour, and at places like Hod Hill, near Stourpaine, I have half expected to find Mr Crabtree around the next tree-lined bend, but perhaps he was fishing elsewhere on the days I was there.

I'm sure barbel would thrive in some of the upstream stretches, but how much attention they would attract is undeterminable.

The River Thames

The Thames is a river I have not fished for many years, but for a while I did spend a lot of time there in search of barbel, concentrating on the area between Windsor and Shepperton. I caught a fair number of fish too, but the Thames is all about location. That applies to all rivers, but on the Thames you can be miles from a 'barbel zone'.

The weir pools make a good start; about eighteen are accessible with a permit from the Environment Agency, which costs around £30. I had great fun on the weir pools; I had an EA permit, and club membership gave access to a couple of other pools. The weir pools are not always easy to fish, as there are often few fishable areas and the river bed can be strewn with rocks. Barbel are present though, and I had a few 'pool' fish, which were challenging and a thrill to catch. It is also worth trying below weir pools where the flow is still good and the fishing is often free. One neglected area that is well worth considering is immediately above a weir pool; the current often picks up in the area and is often favoured by barbel and I have had a few from such areas. Make sure you are not in someone's garden though!

One of the superb swims at Longham

76

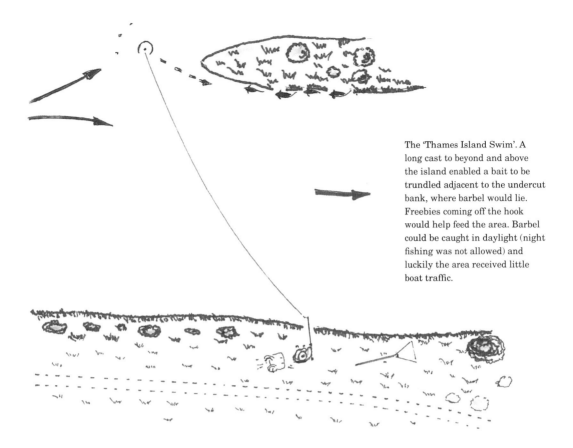

The 'Thames Island Swim'. A long cast to beyond and above the island enabled a bait to be trundled adjacent to the undercut bank, where barbel would lie. Freebies coming off the hook would help feed the area. Barbel could be caught in daylight (night fishing was not allowed) and luckily the area received little boat traffic.

Towpath areas can be worth a try; I often fished such areas on a Monday following a Sunday match, when plenty of bait would have gone in. If you find an area that produces barbel, it is well worth fishing a swim for several successive days, introducing bait on each visit. One swim I fished every evening into darkness for a week. I caught nothing on the first visit, three barbel on the second evening and on the last day of the week I started catching barbel as soon as darkness fell and they stopped feeding at daybreak; I had fourteen in that one night.

Weirs and towpaths apart, the Thames is all about looking for features, whether it's where the river narrows, where tributaries join, bends, bridges and so on.

Islands are very much worth casting a bait to. One of my favourite Thames swims was against an island which was wooded and uninhabited and had undercut banks. My swim was just below the upstream end of the island and my tactic was to whack a meat bait above the island, even beyond it, and to let the bait trundle under control, as close to the island as possible. It worked, and I caught barbel. Often the meat would fly off the hook but land in the right spot, providing a supply of freebies to the area. Baits were large lumps of luncheon meat and liver sausage. Why not put several lumps on the hook length? If at least one stayed on the hook that would work, I thought. I counted the number that came off as the weight landed and if one remained on the hook I was happy. I put more and more pieces of bait on; it looked ridiculous having a 'kebab' of meat lumps eight inches long, but more baits meant more freebies. By chance, on one cast, which was a fair distance, no pieces came off and as soon as the 'kebab' bounced along the island it was taken with a savage pull. A barbel was soon landed. Subsequently I secured the meat pieces the best I could and added a thick stalk of grass on the hook bend. The 'kebab' again landed intact, and the result was the same – another barbel. Incredibly, I was catching barbel on baits eight inches long!

Around that time I was also fishing the River Kennet, and the swim I was concentrating on was on a deepish narrow bend. The river was thick with weed except for the far bank, where the shadow cast from overhanging trees created a weed-free channel. I had been using liver sausage as bait, which resulted in a number of barbel. The thought occurred, why not try a 'kebab-type' bait entirely of liver sausage about eight inches long, just to see if it worked? A gentle underarm cast and splash, and the 'kebab' landed just where I wanted. A few minutes passed and wham, a savage take and a good barbel was hooked. Landing fish in the swim wasn't easy because of the thick weed, but I eventually got it safely in the net, a barbel of about eight pounds in weight. That was probably the last time I used the 'kebab' bait. The liver sausage I was using was a firm type bought in small tubes. It wasn't cheap and casting out a bait that cost a couple of pounds was not exactly economical!

Returning to the Thames, another option is to fish from a boat, which is a wholly different experience. I knew a couple of anglers who were successful using punts and inflatables, the method allowing mobility and access to areas otherwise unfished. I was invited to join a friend who regularly caught barbel from his punt, but boats just aren't my thing.

Big barbel have now been caught from the Thames, but I don't think we will truly discover what secrets it holds.

Thames tributaries

The Thames has many tributaries and most contain barbel. I have fished many of them, but only two seriously for barbel: the Wey and the Kennet.

My fishing on the Wey started well – I had an eight pounder on a Barbel Catchers' Club fish-in – but from thereon things went downhill. I lived not too far from the river, and for a while I spent a fair amount of time in the Wisley to Byfleet area. The free stretch at Byfleet certainly held plenty of barbel, but

A River Wey fish

I didn't find it appealing, as it adjoined a housing estate and the banks were well worn. Wisley was the antithesis, countrified in appearance and rarely a person in sight. I fished the area a number of times, but could not find any barbel. I pre-baited swims, moved around and spent time fish-spotting. I never did catch a barbel there; loads and loads of chub, not big ones, but I never saw a barbel. I just don't think they were there in any number. From what I hear, they are more commonplace now and widespread throughout much of the Wey.

River Kennet

The Kennet is one of our most famous barbel rivers. At 45 miles long (72 km) it is not one of the longest, but barbel are common throughout the river from Reading to Newbury.

I first fished the river many years ago at Aldermaston Mill, where day tickets were and still are available. I was soon drawn to the magnetism of the river; it was enchanting, and I couldn't wait to catch my first Kennet barbel. Reading & District AA controlled much of the lower river and I joined the club at the first opportunity. Names like the Lower Benyons, Upper Benyons, Padworth, Theale and Woolhampton became very familiar to me, as well as the Burghfield Fishery, where I could fish the large pit and the adjacent Kennet, being an RMC bailiff. I caught many fish throughout the river up as far as Woolhampton. The average size wasn't that high,

three, maybe four, pounds, and on one weir pool the barbel didn't exceed a pound. There were always reports of the odd bigger fish being caught on the river, but I never witnessed the capture of any.

Fortunately I managed to get a ticket on a stretch that I had been eager to fish. It was a tremendous fishery with a great variety of swims, full of ranunculus and mostly tree-lined. I walked the banks a couple of times and earmarked a few swims that looked very 'barbelly'. An added bonus was that only one or two others fished the stretch, and one was the bailiff, whom I got to know. I started catching straight away, hard-fighting barbel of seven to eight pounds and eventually nine pounders. Night fishing was banned, but I would sneak an hour into darkness, which proved very successful. The bailiff was also fishing at night and he had no objection to my 'stolen hours', as he was always still fishing himself when I left the car park anyway.

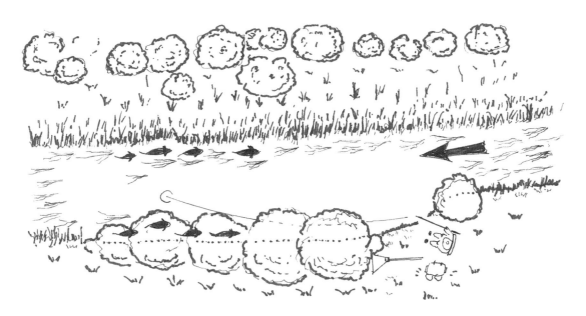

The 'Unfishable Swim'. On arrival each time, a 20ft raft of dead weed had to be cleared before I could fish. An accurate underarm cast under the overhanging trees was necessary to put a bait amongst the barbel, or occasionally a fish could be picked up from the far bank weeded area using a long hook length. Like the majority of swims on the stretch, barbel avoided the deeper open water mid-river. Effectively such areas were 'barbel-free zones', even in the dark, despite the water being very little fished.

Three swims accounted for most of the barbel: the 'unfishable swim', 'the bend' and the 'bat swim'. The unfishable swim was exactly that. It looked great but loose weed accumulated in the pool, occupying a third of the width of the river and making fishing impossible. Undeterred, I spent about half an hour on arrival on each visit dragging much of the weed out so I could get a bait in the water. Casting out, I would have a bite to eat whilst the disturbance subsided, but the inevitable would happen; the rod would almost be wrenched from the rest, resulting in a good barbel. It was very much a daytime swim and I would generally catch on warm, sunny summer afternoons – evenings were quiet. This was the swim where I caught the nine pounders. Strangely I only met two other anglers in the unfishable swim; one was just passing by and I had a chat with him. I bumped into him again on the Avon, only recognising him by his reel. The other was fishing the next swim downstream and I had a brief conversation with him, I met him again later on, on many occasions – he was Fred Crouch, the legendary barbel angler.

The 'Bend' was an evening swim. It had barbel written all over it and I regularly caught fish from it; the average size was bigger than from other swims and I generally caught one or two fish per session. This was the swim where I used my 'kebab' bait, mentioned above.

The 'Bat Swim' was a spot any barbel angler would stop at, yet I never once found anyone fishing it or had a soul pass me by while I was fishing there. It was below a small copse where the river widened slightly, and the water was deep shallowing towards the tail of the pool, where weed extended from bank

The Bend Swim. Barbel hugged the clean channel under the trees on the far bank – landing them in the thickly-weeded 8ft deep swim was far from easy.

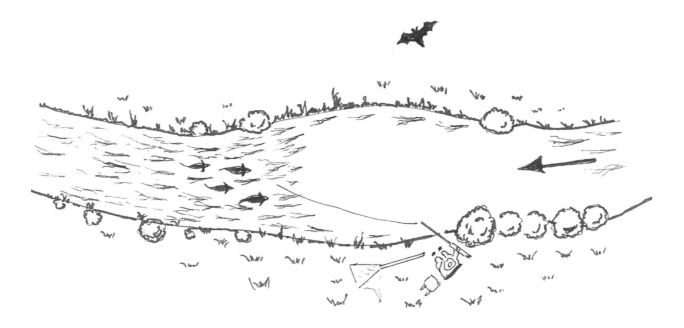

The 'Bat Swim' came to life at nightfall. Bats circled in numbers and barbel began to feed in the densely-weeded shallows downstream. The deep pool never produced a single bite.

to bank. Bushes and small trees fringed the bank downstream. It was so called because of the large numbers of bats that used to appear at dusk. Often I was surrounded by the furry winged creatures, brushing my ears at times and trying to grab my weight or bait as I cast out. Quite eerie!

The river bed was clean gravel. The pool looked an ideal holding area, but I couldn't get a single bite from it. Bait, as always, was a large chunk of meat; liver sausage or luncheon meat. Barbel had to be somewhere, so I tried everywhere in the swim, which was about six feet deep (deep for the stretch).

Thinking of the unfishable and other swims, I often found barbel didn't favour open areas such as the centres of pools, instead preferring the shallower, weedy margins or the tail of the pool. There were definite 'barbel-free zones' just where you would expect to find fish. The shallows below the Bat swim were two feet deep at the most. I walked down the centre of the river one day in the close season, sketching a map of the swim and recording the depths. Perhaps a bait fished in the weedy shallows

might work? I whacked a bait well downstream into the weedy area and fed a little line so the weight and bait could find the bottom. It was dusk and before too long I had a decisive bite. The shallow water meant bringing a barbel back through the weed was not too difficult, and a decent fish was soon in the net. The Bat Swim became a favourite spot, and I continued to catch barbel from the weedy shallows below, though never the pool. I couldn't fish from further downstream because of overhanging branches of the trees and shrubs.

Observation is all important. On one pre-season recce to my Kennet stretch, the only barbel I could find was in the margins above the 'unfishable swim'. I was crawling amongst the rushes no more than 6' from the fish and I could watch it take in a mouthful of silt in 4' of water. Each time it would rise to the surface, blow out the silt and chomp on its meal. It repeated the process as it journeyed upstream. Judging by the number of mozzie bites I got at dusk, I guess bloodworms were on the menu.

The absence of other barbel was a little concerning but finally I found some. Climbing a tree above the 'Bat Swim' I saw a curiously, tightly packed shoal of decent fish, barely moving. They occupied an area no larger than that of a medium car. I could roughly count them – there were sixty.

Further upstream of the Bat Swim the river was much shallower, and barbel could be seen but none were particularly large. After dark sucking and slurping sounds came from everywhere, as barbel were feeding on the surface. They were difficult to see, but it looked like some were feeding upside down. I tried to catch one using a floating bait, but failed.

There were other swims on the stretch, of course, and I caught a few fish from them. One deep hole looked very interesting, but I never caught a single barbel, summer or winter, from it, just a few chub. There is no doubt that barbel favour certain areas which are to their liking, but these are not always apparent to the angler.

Moving to Christchurch meant that it was no longer feasible to fish the River Kennet, and with deep regret I fished the river for the last time before the move. I fished the Bend Swim, failing to get a single bite, and left with sadness. My affection with the Kennet did not end there, however, for I drove up to Aldermaston Mill of all places, at a later date, for a fish-in and social event with the Barbel Catchers. and on that occasion a decent barbel graced my landing net.

BIG BARBEL

The barbel record was shared by three fish for a long time at 14lbs 6oz, the first caught from the Thames at Molesey in 1888 by Mr T. Wheeler and the other two from the Royalty Fishery in 1934 (Mr H.D. Tryon) and 1937 (Mr F.W. Wallis). Mr Wallis also caught a 14lb 4oz barbel from the Royalty. These three Royalty fish were all caught in the month of September.

The famous Railway Pool, scene of the capture of the old barbel record

It is only a personal view, but I have always regarded the next record barbel as being C.H. Cassey's fish of 16lb 1oz caught from the Hampshire Avon in 1960, until it was surpassed by Pete Woodhouse's 16lb 2oz fish in 1994. In defence of Mr Cassey's fish, it was caught whilst salmon fishing and in the coarse fishing season, and it was weighed by the bailiff. I spoke to the bailiff, Bunny Collins, years later on the riverbank and he told me of the weighing. It registered well above sixteen pounds, but I think the scales only had four or eight-ounce divisions, and the one ounce was added as a nominal figure, though it may have been an ounce or two more. It was rejected as a record because it was foul-hooked. Where in the body it was foul-hooked I don't know, but if the lure was an artificial minnow say, foul-hooking would be quite likely if the barbel was trying to grab it. The whole idea of having a record list is to show what big fish have been landed using a rod and line. Foul-hooking is unfortunate, but should not be used as grounds for disqualification. Sure, it should be mentioned on the list if that is the case.

We also had the silly rejection of the old 14lb 6oz records, and a lower qualification weight was introduced. No further comment necessary! That was followed by the rejection of Jason Bailey's fish of 15lb 11oz from the River Wey in the early 1990s. Jason's fish, I believe, was genuine. He had an independent witness, but despite further evidence of the capture, he was not even contacted by the Record Fish Committee.

Events changed anyway with the emergence of big fish from the Severn, Wensum and Great Ouse in the late 1990s, with barbel to over seventeen pounds. We thought at the time that they might go on to twenty pounds, a prophesy that came true. They have since reached perhaps 21lbs plus.

The current record is Grahame King's 21lb 1oz Great Ouse fish caught in 2006. I heard a slightly bigger fish, an ounce heavier, was caught on the River Wensum but wasn't satisfactorily witnessed, though I can't fully confirm the details of that capture. What I find most surprising is the number of 'super barbs' reported from different rivers in recent times. Some of the rivers I have not even heard of. In part it reflects the number of rivers that now hold barbel following widespread stocking.

The record list, although showing some magnificent fish caught, doesn't totally reflect a true picture of each river. There is a dichotomy of considerations; firstly a number of big fish, maybe even river records, are kept quiet and not reported, and secondly a few big fish may be confined to one small area, giving a false impression of the river's overall potential.

Another observation is the date of the capture of each river record. Almost every fish has been caught in the 21st century, as if barbel weren't about before the turn of the millennium!

I have a rough idea of the size and population of barbel in my local Hampshire Avon and to a lesser extent the Dorset Stour. There has been a size increase in both rivers, probably more so in the case of the Stour. The biggest surprise to me, though, is the current size of Kennet fish. There are big barbel throughout the river now, and club records range from fifteen to nearly nineteen pounds. Truly staggering! The 19lb 5oz river record caught by Duncan Kellett in 2006 looked amazing and was in superb condition. Every entry in the river record list just shows how barbel have thrived throughout England and Wales in recent years. May it long continue.

I'm unqualified to write about other rivers. I've seen many pictures, videos and TV programmes about some and they look great. Parts of the Nene could have been mistaken for the Kennet, and the River Trent looks terrific.

One other river justifies a mention and that is the Taff, in Wales of course. I have never seen the river, but I watched with interest a series on TV about the Taff, presented by renowned writer and angler Will Millard. The River Taff was severely polluted and ran black as a result of the coal mining industry. It was lifeless and declared biologically dead. When the deep mined pits closed it devastated the working communities in the area, but one bonus was an improvement in the state of the river. Now it runs clear and has a healthy stock of fish: salmon, trout, grayling and barbel. Will caught salmon, trout and grayling on the programme, but the barbel didn't oblige. Yet to date, barbel have been caught to 19lb 2oz – staggering! Could a once lifeless river provide the next record barbel?

Why are we seeing such 'super whiskers'? They have been turning up throughout England and Wales; we have seen twenty-pounders from the Great Ouse, Wensum and Ivel now, and maybe other rivers. The River Ivel twenty-one pounder was killed by an otter I understand, a tragedy. The Environment Agency's comment on the death was unbelievable – they said it was unhealthy just to have a few big fish chased by a handful of anglers and there should be a range of fish from small to large. Whilst I would agree that we should have different year classes of barbel in our rivers and fish of different weights, they failed to recognise the significance of a truly noteworthy barbel, one of historic importance.

I don't know why we are getting such large barbel; my guess is likely to be no better than anyone else's. Perhaps it is a combination of factors. Certainly barbel are more widespread, having been stocked in rivers with healthy, hatchery-reared fish which might otherwise do better than native stock. Perhaps the average weight of these stocked fish will exceed the norm for rivers with naturally-bred barbel? Certainly stocked trout will outgrow their natural brethren in rivers.

The climate must play its part as well. The summer of 2018 illustrated how much warmer it has been and the winters in the south of England have been noticeably milder; on only four nights last winter did the temperature fall to just below zero. Don't most species grow to a larger size in the warmer climes of the Continent?

There is also the question of accessibility; on the Hampshire Avon when the river was reputed to hold some very big barbel, what chance was there of one being caught? Much of the river was only open from July to the end of January, even less in some cases. And night fishing? You could forget about it, as on most fisheries you had to make a dash for the car park at dusk. Also the number of tickets was severely restricted in places.

Tackle is another consideration. Today's barbel anglers will be well equipped and lines of suitable strength and reliability will be used, hooks too. I cannot imagine the number of big fish that were lost years ago due to inferior tackle; some thought being 'smashed up' by a big fish was a badge of honour. Hook a big barbel nowadays and there is every chance you will land it, if you are sensible enough.

Many attribute the big barbel phenomenon to the bait used by the modern angler. Highly nutritional pellet baits are widely used, not only as bait but as feed as well. There is no doubt such baits promote high growth rates. They are, after all, used to increase the growth of fish in hatcheries and fish farms. Halibut pellets are a great favourite, with high levels of oil and protein. Boilies and paste baits too are highly nutritional, with some specially made for the barbel angler.

Of course, the paramount factor is water quality. There is no doubt some improvements have been made to many rivers, but more needs to be done. A lot comes down to cost, and government agencies, industries and landowners don't have the funding to carry out full upgrades. And the demand for water has never been so great; we are using more individually and the uncontrolled population growth just continues.

So will the record remain at 21lb 1oz, or will it be bettered? It's a good few years now since the current record fish was caught and the big Wensum fish last appeared, so perhaps they are no longer around, or past their peak. I remember many years ago some predicted that the next record would come from the Royalty or Throop, which is still possible but not that likely, as the present heavyweights on those fisheries have a fair way to go. Yet in a sense they were right, as they have both gone on to surpass the old record.

It may be that one of the emergent rivers is capable of producing a new record, such as the Taff already mentioned or perhaps the River Dove, which is one of the most recent to produce a river record. An 18lb 6oz Dove fish was caught in October 2014, so it would have the potential to reach twenty-plus in the winter months by now.

Perhaps though, Old Father Thames will have the final say. The river has for a long time been famed for its barbel fishing and let's not forget it once held the record. Stories can be recollected of a Mr Webb of Reading, a commercial fisherman and a keen barbel angler, who caught some fine specimen barbel before and during the Second World War. He firmly believed there were twenty-pound barbel in the Thames and he once lost a fish at the net which he thought was around that weight from the River Kennet near Reading. That twenty-pound barrier was finally broken in 2018 and I understand the biggest Thames barbel is now ranked number three in the all-time record list. It is not inconceivable that we may see even bigger barbel coming from the Thames in the future.

In any event, I'm sure before this book is published some of the records I have listed will already be out of date. No doubt a Mr Green of Northumberland will have caught a twenty-three pounder fly fishing on the River Tyne, but it will have been rejected by the Record Committee because it was caught two days before the coarse season opened.

The captors of big fish mentioned have all been male, but I should give credit to the young lady who caught one of the biggest barbel from the Avon, a sixteen-pound-plus fish – well done. Well done also to all the captors of records and river records past and present.

AVON GALLERY

A selection of some of the barbel that have graced my landing net over the years

A chunky September fish

Caught first cast, just before the sun began to set

A meat caught fish from under the rod tip in January

January fish caught on static bait

Floodwater time

One of the many from a narrow gap swim

Another fish from the margins in a severely-flooded river

A big January fish on flavoured meat, when a strong wind whipped up foot high waves on the river

Late afternoon in the Royalty 'House Pool' produced this scale-perfect barbel

Another
customer for
a roving bait

Colourful, fin and scale perfect – a beautiful-looking fish

A large September fish tempted by sweetcorn just before nightfall

One of a pair of big fish that moved around together

A big winter fish on a home-made bait

The fish I had been waiting for – caught on an upstream bait in the margins

A big winter barbel with a liking for sweet-flavoured meat

THE ROACH

The roach, scientific name *Rutilus rutilus*, also known as the common roach, is one of our favourite fish and one of the commonest. It is widespread throughout England, Wales, Northern Ireland and parts of Scotland. It is also found in much of Europe and Western Asia, but in this chapter I will solely write about roach in the UK.

The roach is, of course, a member of the Cyprinidae, the carp family if you like. It is found in most waters, from small brooks to major rivers and tiny ponds to large reservoirs. It is less likely to be found in small fast-flowing upland streams.

The roach is not a big fish; most will easily fit in the palm of the hand. When I was a teenager on club outings, they had to be measured for the weigh-in at the end of the day; an eight-inch fish, that is to the tip of the tail, was the minimum length for weighing and was considered a sizeable fish or more colloquially a 'goer'. On some outings many roach could be caught, but perhaps you would only have one fish to trouble the weighmaster. An eight-inch fish would generally weigh around four ounces, a nice size for the species. A pound roach is a big fish and a two-pounder a real specimen.

I have a glass-cased roach on my living room wall, not a stuffed fish but a very realistic glass fibre facsimile. It measures about sixteen inches to the fork of the tail and I would guess it would represent a fish weighing two and three quarter pounds, an enormous roach. Otherwise I have no knowledge of the length to weight ratio.

Small roach are very gregarious; as juveniles they will start by eating plankton and then move on to small insects as they grow. They are slimmer in size at that stage and lack the colouration of mature fish, which have a proportionally greater depth. A net of very small roach, dace and chub of similar size can look very alike as the roach lack the colouration and distinct body shape of an adult. Mature roach

My glass fibre roach

golden in colour and there are distinct differences between the species. The roach has a protruding upper lip, reflecting the fact that the roach is inclined to be a bottom-feeding fish, while the rudd is more of a surface feeder. Also the roach has a red eye in comparison to the yellow eye of the rudd. The inclination for roach to feed on the bottom is not totally definitive, for they will at times feed happily at mid-depth or even on the surface; likewise rudd often feed on the bottom.

with their bright red fins will stand out in a mixed bag of fish, hence their nickname of redfins.

A small adult roach of seven inches, say, is a very attractive fish. It will have the fully-developed colouration of eyes, fins and body. A mature fish is a palette of colours. The eyes will be reddish and the defined-rayed fins bright red in colour, though slightly darker in the dorsal and tail fins. The body ranges in colour from green at the top to white underneath with silverish flanks with a hint of blue. The scales are well defined, more evidently so in the more mature fish. Some time ago a survey of Thames roach aged an eight-inch fish at ten years; an Avon fish would have likely achieved the same length in half the time. Roach, it is understood, reach a maximum age in the middle teens, eighteen years supposedly being the limit.

I have been lucky enough to witness and catch some very big roach and they are truly magnificent fish. There does seem to be a variation in the colour and shape of the big redfins. Some are rounder in body shape with almost metallic blue flanks, others are flatter sided and lacking the blueish colour.

There is a similarity between roach and rudd (*Scardinius erythrophthalmus*), but a rudd is more

The only big redfin of the day, but worth its weight in saffron

Hybridisation can make roach identification problematic, and hybrids occur between a number of species. I once caught a roach-like fish in the dark whilst tench fishing. It weighed 4lb 7oz, but upon close examination, the anal fin which was too bream-like. In fact later examination of the photographs showed it to be a rudd x bream hybrid. Strangely I never caught either a rudd or a bream from the lake.

Identification of a roach-bream hybrid is usually not difficult. The hybrid is deeper bodied than a true roach, the colour is paler and the fins are not red. More significantly the anal fin is more bream-like, ie longer. There is also the question of second-generation hybrids, where a fish may be 75% true roach. Identification becomes more difficult with second generation and it does seem that a DNA test is required to establish the true genetics of a fish. I have no expertise in the matter, but to me, if a fish looks very much like a roach, it is a roach. Roach also hybridise with rudd and bleak, I understand, though I have never knowingly witnessed one. If there is any indication that a fish may not be a true roach, say in colouration, fin shape or body shape, then I will consider it to be a hybrid of some sort.

The colour of roach, like all fish, appears to be dependent partly upon habitat. A roach from a murky canal or pond will likely be pale in colour as opposed to a pristine, vividly-coloured roach from a clear chalk stream such as the River Test, but it is the same fish - a roach is a roach is a roach.

Ron Smith with one of his 3lb roach

The roach is easy to hold in the hand. The prominent rays of the fins are not hard and the body is not as muscular as that of a game fish, such as a trout or small salmon. There are no teeth in the mouth; it has pharyngeal (throat) teeth, which are arranged in a single row. The mouth is small, as it generally feeds on small invertebrates and flora on the river or lake bed, therefore hooks and baits need to be small, though a big roach is quite capable of taking a small boilie or a thumbnail-size piece of bread flake.

Mick Connelly with a fine 2lb roach

Roach spawn in April or May. I was once lucky enough to see them spawning on the Kennet and Avon Canal in late May or even early June; there were hundreds if not thousands of fish present. It was an incredible sight to witness. On all the occasions I walked along that stretch of the canal before and after that spawning, I never saw a single roach.

Roach, to me at least, are a special fish. I don't know if it stems from the time when I was a tiny tot; my first fish at the age of five or six was either a roach or a gudgeon and I certainly caught roach at that age. Perhaps I even knew what a roach was by the time I started school!

I have seen big fish of most species, barbel, carp, pike, tench and salmon, but to me a big roach is the most impressive fish. I have heard of anglers playing very big redfins and bringing them to the surface only to have the hook pull out. How heart-breaking that must be. Fortunately it has never happened to me with the few big roach I have hooked.

In this chapter I will aim to write about roach in general, but the emphasis will be on my experiences on the Hampshire Avon and the styles I have adopted in pursuit of big fish.

The approach

Most of what I have written about the approach to barbel fishing also applies to roach. Preparation is vitally important in any form of angling, whatever the species. Get it right and you are much more likely to enjoy a fruitful day on the riverbank or by the lake.

Ensure your tackle is in good condition and complete. Make sure your bait containers and buckets have been thoroughly cleaned and all the mud has been scraped off your boots and they have been washed. A laundry bag is ideal for keeping your footwear in the car boot.

Keep a diary and list all your outings. Record the date, where you fished and the start and finish times. List the number of fish caught and the weights of the better fish, if only estimates. Many roach anglers may aim for a target net of fish, so by all means add an estimate weight of your day's catch if you wish. Record the weather conditions; the wind direction, the air and water temperatures if you can, or just a comment if it has been a cold, mild or hot day, or sunny or cloudy. I have a habit of putting my hand in the water on arrival; it is a quick guide to see if the water is a favourable temperature.

Water is at its densest at about four degrees Celsius (39° Fahrenheit). The late great Dick Walker once wrote that roach can be very hard to catch below that temperature, but I think that can be self-defeating, as roach can still be caught at such times and it is always worth a try. It is worth knowing though that roach will move into deeper water once the surface water does reach that sort of temperature.

A second diary is also worth keeping. Thoughts can be recorded; maps of your venue can be drawn, showing weed beds and depths. A bank-high river in winter can look very different from what you saw on a warm summer day. It helps if you know what you are fishing over. You may visit a match venue one day and witness a good bag of roach caught by an angler at a certain peg, then return in winter when the peg numbers have gone and the bare trees give little indication as to where you saw the catch made. It follows that it is worth carrying a small notebook and pen in your jacket pocket, so you can make notes on the bank, draw maps and update your diary at a later date.

As I wrote earlier, it is also worthwhile keeping a card in your diary of your reels and line strengths and noting when you replaced the line and adding a number each time you have used that spool, not forgetting to replace the line after a number of days' usage or a period of time.

Write in your diary where you plan to fish for the forthcoming months and decide where you are going to fish before you leave home, not on the road. By all means adopt plan B and change venue if you find on arrival that conditions are not to your liking or even that there is a match on. Also don't forget your tackle list; check it well beforehand to make sure everything is ready, and take a last-minute look before you go outside the front door. A bait box of maggots or a packed lunch is no good to you if left in the fridge or on the kitchen counter. It is easily done.

Tackle

Before detailing tackle, I must reiterate the

significance of stealth. Avoid highly-glossed rods – if necessary give them a coat of matt varnish. Clothing should be sombre in colour, ideally olive green or khaki. Don't use an orange or white bucket for your groundbait. Even a green one can be glossy, so pick a dull green or camouflage-coloured one. The same applies to bait containers. Landing net frames and handles, bank sticks and chair legs should not be silver in colour; paint them matt green if they are. Sit well back from the water's edge; those open, often-fished swims should be fished from an out-of-sight position behind nearby rushes or shrubbery.

I nearly always stand when float fishing for roach on rivers, which means I am more likely to be conspicuous, but I always try to stand back from the edge and look for some sort of cover if possible. I try to avoid sudden movements and keep as quiet as possible.

Rods

My progression in choice of rods and other tackle for roach has followed that of my barbel gear. It has very much been related to the development of tackle over the years as well as my budget at the time. As a lad I started with different cane rods, which to a large extent served their purpose. For a while, perhaps one summer, I tried a cane pole on my local canal, but I found it wasn't for me. It had to be a rod and reel, a cheap fixed-spool (an Intrepid) at the time. Once I started work and could afford better tackle I bought an Avon rod (Davenport & Fordham) for roach and other species, mostly for the Hampshire Avon. I still possess it and very occasionally still use it. Elsewhere I continued to use a longer split cane rod that had served me well.

With the introduction of glass fibre, I progressed to a 14ft rod, an Auger, which I used mainly on the River Thames. It was a great rod on the Thames and

I had some good catches of redfins using it.

My next two rods for roach I got at the same time from my local tackle dealer, Cliff Glenton, a great angler and a great character. They were both Hardy rods: a 12ft Matchmaker and a slightly shorter F J Taylor Trotter. The Matchmaker became my standard rod for the River Avon, to which I had switched my roach fishing. I had some good roach using it, including my first two-pounders, and the rod was light enough to use all day.

Along came carbon rods and I invested in a 13ft Shimano XMS 39. Apart from not having a screw-lock reel fitting, it is a brilliant roach rod; it has a through action and is ultra slim. The blank has a maximum width of half an inch (12mm). I don't feel the need ever to replace it.

Any rod between twelve and sixteen feet is fine as long as it has the right action and you are comfortable using it. Length is not too important; it is largely a matter of personal choice.

The choice of rod is not easy these days for the newcomer. It is difficult to gauge the action of a rod in the confines of a tackle shop. I have tested rods for magazine reviews and some have been budget price, others expensive, but in all cases the only way to test the rod has been to use it on the riverbank. Expensive rods tend to be slimmer and lighter and are likely the best option, but avoid a rod with a 'tippy' action, which in my opinion, will not be suitable for roach on either river or stillwater. Moreover, many rods will have a 'commercial' label, meaning they are aimed at the stillwater stocked with carp, which are so popular these days. That's probably not the rod you want for roach. Personally I would look for a rod with a 'Match' label. Read the angling magazine test reviews and advert descriptions and seek the advice of your tackle dealer. A budget rod will cost as little as £25, while expensive rods start at about £100. The choice is not easy; take your time before deciding.

I have a pair of Harrison Advanced quiver rods; they are super sensitive and light. I've attached isotopes to the tips of both rods. Having detachable butts, they are not too long in the bag and easily fit in the car boot. I tend not to use them very much, preferring to float-fish. They come into their own when the river is high or in flood and the swims are more confined. I find eleven feet about right for a quiver rod for roach. There are plenty on the market, but as I wrote in the barbel chapters you only need one tip, ideally already spliced into the rod. You don't need all those extra tips in your rod quiver bag; you're an angler, not an archer.

Cane rods made by specialists are beautifully crafted, though they do come at a price. They are okay up to about twelve feet and fine on most rivers, but at thirteen feet and above they are a little heavy and not as responsive as a carbon rod. By all means use the longer ones if you are comfortable in handling them, but for me a longer rod has to be carbon, even if it is, sadly, a Far Eastern import. Pragmatism rules, I'm afraid.

The Ryobi GR; perfect fixed-spool reels for roach

Reels

When using quiver rods, fixed-spools will be my only choice. My old Ryobi GR series reels are perfect. They are light in weight (8oz/225g) and compact, and the wind is very smooth and the retrieve rate good.

I used fixed-spools when float fishing for many years. My now-replaced Mitchell 408s served me well; the only fault was not having a manually-closing bale arm. The tweak on the line caused by turning the handle to close the bale arm caused the loss over the years of several fish which I could ill afford to lose. Once I bought my Ryobi reels with manual closing bale arms, the problem never occurred again. As long as fixed-spool reels are light and compact and not too flashy in colour, they should be fine for float fishing.

The Speedia – simplistic, yet the ideal centre-pin for roach

It took me longer to switch to centre-pin reels for float fishing for roach, as the models I tried just weren't to my liking. Initially, budget reels were plainly not free running enough and the Match Aerial, which was used by some, had problems. The diameter was too large, the drum width too narrow and the spool too shallow. These faults combined to cause the line to wrap around the foot all too easily. Somewhere I saw a Speedia reel, and I managed to get one from an antique tackle trader. The reel was perfectly designed: four inches in diameter, a deep spool with just the right width. It also had a strong easy-to-use ratchet. I still use my Speedia now for float fishing for roach on rivers, as you can't improve on perfection! New, well-made centre-pins are available today; opt for one with a four-inch diameter, light in weight and free-running, with a deeper drum for better control.

Casting

With the Speedia, casting is not really a problem, for I don't fish at any distance. Usually I pull off a couple of loops of line from between the first couple of rings and that is enough to cast the distance I want. Inadvertently, one day, out of force of habit, I cast off the side of the Speedia, as if I were using my wide drum Aerials for barbel, and amazingly it worked. In theory it shouldn't have, as it was like casting with a half-empty fixed-spool. So any time now I want to trot a float mid-river, I cast off the side of the reel. Only rarely does it fail.

Lines

A good quality line is always essential and the finer the diameter for the breaking strain the better. With most species the line strength will be less than the size of fish sought, but that's not usually the case with roach (and dace) in particular. It is very unlikely that you will be broken by a roach, even a big one, unless your line is old and not been cared for. A 4lb bs line is possible when ledgering; I would use a 3lb or 4lb line depending on conditions and tie directly onto the hook. Float fishing is a different matter; use a 4lb line and you are unlikely to get many bites, so 3lb is the maximum strength I would use. On other occasions, when the water is clear, especially in the summer, I would likely use a 2lb or 2.5lb line and possibly an even lighter hook length of 1.8lb.

That applies to rivers; on a stillwater I would use a minimum of 2lb breaking strain.

I always use Maxima Chameleon as a main line. It is available in all breaking strains: 1lb, 1.5lb, 2lb, 2.5lb, 3 and 4lb. If I use a lighter hook length, I use a finer diameter make. My favourite was Bayer Ultima 1.8lb (0.10mm), though I'm not sure if the same brand is still available. Comparing brands nowadays is difficult, as some are labelled in pounds whilst others are listed by diameter. The best bet is to select two or three brands recommended by your tackle dealer and give each one a test on the bank.

Hooks

Hook strength is less important for roach; let's face it, you are not going to have your hook straightened out by a redfin (or are you?) I wouldn't use a very fine wire hook or a spade end for that matter. I've

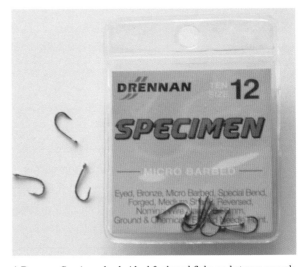

A Drennan Specimen hook, ideal for bread flake and strong enough for an unexpected barbel or carp

landed too many big fish, particularly barbel, and found small, fine hooks or spades embedded in the fish's lip. I wouldn't advise anyone to use a spade end hook, but that is only a personal view.

I only use Drennan Specimen hooks, micro-barbed or barbless, for roach; they are reasonably fine yet strong. They are available down to size 20, I believe. Drennan also market a Sweetcorn hook, down to size 16 and a wide gape Specialist, which goes down to a size 18. I've yet to try either. I did try some Kamasan hooks once, when my tackle dealer was out of Drennan Specimens in the size I wanted, and I found them very similar to Drennan Specimens. I use just three sizes of hook for roach: size 16 for maggots, size 14 for sweetcorn and size 12 for bread. With a bread punch I would use a size 16 hook, but I haven't used a punch for years. Somewhere in my tackle box there are some size 18s for using maggots when the going gets tough, but I don't recall the last time I used them.

Knots

I use only two knots when roach fishing, but most of the time it is just one and that is the universal knot, which I described in the barbel chapters. To reiterate, in simple terms, I pass the line through the hook eye, make a loop with the loose end, then with the end of the line I wind it back along the line above the hook and one side of the loop at the same time. Four turns is enough, add saliva and tighten the knot. Trim off the end.

The other knot is for tying on a hook length. I've never found the perfect knot for tying two lengths of line together. The customary knots illustrated in most books, ie the tucked-in blood knot type, are not safe. Tying two universal knots against each other does work, but I am not totally happy with it. The ideal knot for joining two lines, especially of different breaking strains, has to be the loop knot, which is not entirely tidy but is secure. There may well be other knots serving the purpose, but I am not familiar with them.

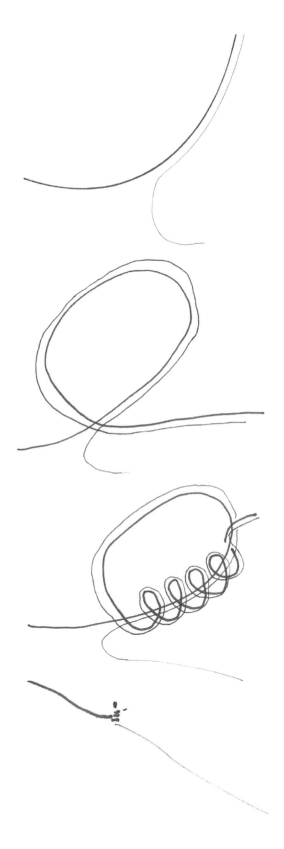

The customary knots illustrated in most books, i.e the tucked-in blood knot type, are not safe. Tying two universal knots against each other does work but I am not totally happy with it. The ideal knot for joining two lines, especially of different breaking strains, has to be the loop knot, which is not entirely tidy but is secure

The loop knot is easy to tie; simply hold the main line and hook length together and make a loop with the ends of the joined two lines, then wrap them around the loop four or five times and pull tight, adding a little saliva. Trim the loose end.

I used to make a loop knot with just the main line to make a paternoster, but the thought of a possible breakage and a fish dragging a weighted line around has put me off the method. I now only use a sliding weight on the line.

When ledgering I use a sliding link, which I make myself. A double-holed sliding bead has a two to two-and-a-half-inch link line tied to a snap lock swivel. A thin green silicon tubing covers the link line and one end of the flattened swivel eyes.

Weights are easily interchangeable using the snap swivel; I use very small Arlesey bombs, as little as one eighth of an ounce. Alternatively a feeder could easily be attached if you so desire. Additionally the snap lock swivel can be used to attach a small bait dropper, if you are using one.

For a link ledger stop I use a 4mm bead or even a micro bead. Passing the line three times through the bead should be enough to secure it in place, four times definitely will.

Floats and shotting

Reels and floats are the two items of tackle that fascinate me the most. Handmade floats are a delight to handle and use, especially the cork-bodied Avon floats, which I'm almost afraid to use. A float was

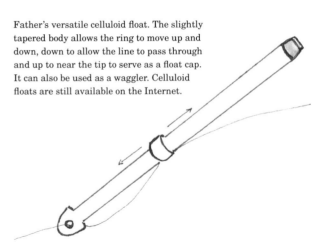

permanently attached to my late father's rod; it was the only one he had as far as I know. Yet it was a very versatile float and would have served well on the local canal or in the Royal Park ponds where we would occasionally fish for roach on family weekend outings. I still vividly remember the float; it was white celluloid with a red tip. The float body tapered slightly towards the eyed bottom and a sliding float cap ring could be slid up and down the body, tightening the line near the tip and loose enough when at the bottom to pass line through. Simple yet clever.

Father's versatile celluloid float. The slightly tapered body allows the ring to move up and down, down to allow the line to pass through and up to near the tip to serve as a float cap. It can also be used as a waggler. Celluloid floats are still available on the Internet.

One day when I was a boy, a superb quill float in my local tackle shop window grabbed my attention. As I was drooling over it, a voice came from behind – "What you looking at, Colin?" It came from a friend of the family and a colleague of my father, a man called Harry Fincham; I knew him well. I pointed out the glorious float and said how good I thought it was. Harry went into the shop and bought it for me, and I very gladly accepted; I was fourteen at the time. You don't forget things like that.

106

I don't carry a huge variety of floats these days and tend to use the same handful. They range from wagglers, onion-bodied floats and drift beaters (also known as wind beaters) for stillwaters and Avons, loafers, and cork-bodied floats for running waters. I must admit I don't like stick floats or wagglers for river fishing; the former have too little of the tip showing for my liking and wagglers are difficult to control. Stick floats do work very well for some, perhaps where the flow is not so great and the river bed fairly even, but on the rivers I fish the flow is that much greater and the river bed undulating. I have seen wagglers used to perfection on slower-flowing rivers, but they are not my preference.

I used to make my own floats, mostly of balsa wood. At times I would make them in batches of up to eighty in one go. The finished article looked good, they were well painted and varnished and proved waterproof, only they never quite performed as intended in faster water. One of the problems at the time was getting all the necessary materials to perfect the ideal float, and also lack of time meant I stopped making them. More on floats later.

For shot, I use a six-division dispenser and buy a few extra tubs of the sizes I use most, which are SSG, AAA, and to a lesser extent BB and no. 6. I've tried most makes and they are all generally okay. The only ones I don't like are those which are too deeply cut, which makes alignment more difficult. Round or oval shot? I don't think there is much difference, but I don't like the bright silver-coloured ones.

Olivettes – I like the bigger ones, as they can save having a line of shot. Somewhere I've got some jumbo ones, big enough to anchor a small boat! I've only got one float big enough to support them. I've never tried small olivettes.

A small dropper is handy; you may be trotting in a steady line with maggots or casters say and a regular deposit of the same bait will prove enticing for roach. Some smaller ones have a small cork insert on the back allowing the hook to be temporarily inserted and can be employed every few casts. Most tackle shops should stock them; otherwise a small (2oz) Seymo tear drop dropper can be bought by mail order from the Tackle Box in Dartford and Chapmans Angling of Hull sell a variety of droppers.

Catapults are invaluable for feeding bait and groundbait; I usually carry a small pouched one.

Other essentials

A disgorger is a must. Keep it handy, such as in your bait box, or hang it around your neck if you are catching regularly. Forceps are also a must; it is

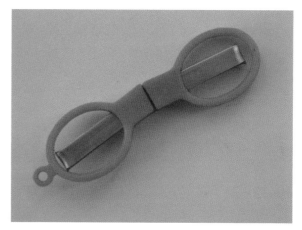

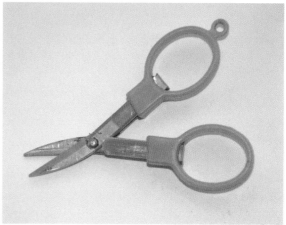

Folding scissors, available for a few quid online.

inevitable that other species will be caught and they will be essential for hook removal. The small curved types are best. Forceps are also useful for attaching shot on the line.

When standing to fish for roach I always use a waist apron. It has a quick-fit snap lock waist band and a two-division pouch; in one half I keep my bait and in the other, tackle odds and ends.

A small towel (green) will help keep your hands clean and dry. Hands do tend to get dirty with different baits and groundbait.

A plummet is essential for determining the depth, especially if the water is still or slow-moving. I prefer the type with cork inserts so they can easily be hooked on. Three eighths or half an ounce will do. I'm not so keen on the spring-loaded type, which fit over a shot; they are convenient but may risk damaging the line.

Scissors are necessary, as knots need trimming. I keep one pair in my tackle box and a pair that folds and closes for safety. It will stay in my jacket pocket or may be transferred to my apron when necessary.

A hook-sharpening stone, kept in a plastic sleeve, always stays in my tackle box

Floats can be delicate and need protection. I keep two different float tubes in the car, one containing those intended solely for rivers and the other for stillwaters.

Feeders are best fished free-running on a link. There are numerous types on the market, from caged and maggot feeders to open-ended ones. They come in different sizes and weights, heavier ones being required for wider rivers or distance casting on stillwaters. Ideally a selection is best, but after choosing your venue and style of feeder fishing, just a few need to be carried in your box to save on weight and space. Give each a try and see what works best. There is no denying how effective and popular feeders are these days.

For weighing roach, in most cases I use my Avons, though I do sometimes carry a tubular spring balance weighing up to eleven pounds, which is accurate and useful when aiming to travel light. A small, fine-mesh net from a landing net serves well for weighing roach. A thick green plastic sheet always stays in my rucksack and I use it in the absence of an unhooking mat for putting the landing net on; it offers protection for the fish and keeps them clean.

A reminder about unhooking mats – fishery rules may insist you have one. You may not need one if you are catching smaller roach, but I've known fellow anglers to be thrown off a fishery for not having one.

I don't use keepnets any more, though I don't see anything wrong with them, providing the fish are carefully placed in the net and the catch released without lifting the net out of the water at the end of the session.

I always travel as light as possible, but invariably I have to use my rucksack because of the bulky photographic gear that I always carry. A quiver holds my rod, landing net, light brolly and bank sticks, most of which have rod rests screwed in. I carry a light chair, which is clipped onto my rucksack. My hands are free to carry a plastic bucket holding mostly groundbait.

The chair I will probably use to put my bucket on with groundbait made up; otherwise I will hang the bucket from a stout extended bank stick and rod rest to avoid bending. Avoid bending down to the ground when standing to get to your groundbait, as you will surely soon get backache if you do. Match anglers' tackle boxes are useful – you can put your bucket and bait on them – but they are somewhat uncomfortable to carry any distance or in negotiating stiles.

Landing nets shouldn't be too small, despite roach not being a large fish; you don't want to be chasing a possible fish of a lifetime, should you hook one, with a tiny net. The exception being if the water only holds small fish, in which case a smaller net will suffice. I use the same landing net for all my fishing, a 32" Fastnet; it is reassuring to know a big roach can be netted at the first attempt and if I want to take a photo, I merely keep the net in the water on a rod rest whilst I fetch the camera and weighing gear.

Waterproof clothing, as already mentioned, is absolutely vital, and don't forget a hat and polarising glasses, two pairs if the budget allows; darker grey for the bright days of summer and amber for duller days and winter.

Finally, two other tackle items that will come in handy when roach fishing on rivers. The first is a length of float tubing, and make sure it fits your float tips – blue is the best colour. The other item is Plasticine or modelling clay; a 500-gram block will cost about three pounds and should last you 25 years. I use dark brown, but a dull green will do. The purchase of these two items is the best tip I can give to a float angler, and they cost little to buy. More on their application later.

Baits

Roach will naturally take all sorts of insects, crustaceans and plant material. The bait will have to be dinky because of the small mouth of the roach, but a very large roach is quite capable of taking a thumbnail-size sample.

The main baits will include maggots, bread, hempseed, tares, small worms and bloodworms, sweetcorn, wheat, cheese, pellets and berries. All other cooked seeds and insects have no doubt been tried and proved successful in the past.

Maggots in their many forms have to be the number one bait; roach love the little wriggly fellows and the not-so-wriggly form, the chrysalis stage, or casters as we anglers know them. A pint of maggots will cost about the same as a bottle of beer and will often be enough for a roach session. At times I've got away with just half a pint for a session, yet years ago I would have taken a gallon for a long day's roaching on the Hampshire Avon. Maggots can be bought in a variety of colours; my preference has been for plain white with a sprinkling of coloured ones thrown in.

I have never tried artificial maggots, but I have tried dead maggots once or twice; they do seem popular with some stillwater anglers when used with feeders.

Casters are a little more expensive than maggots but roach, especially bigger ones, will take them in preference. A pint is plenty for a session and they can be effectively used in conjunction with other baits for feed such as maggots, hemp and tares. They can also be used effectively on the top, especially in stillwaters, once they have developed to the stage where they float.

Bread is another top bait for roach. It can be used in a small form using a bread punch or as a pinch of bread flake on the hook. Breadcrust is not often used for roach and I have only used it for other species. I only use sliced bread for roach; white, thin sliced if available, otherwise medium sliced is fine. A loaf is more than enough for a session; the remainder can be taken home and put in the freezer for groundbait on the next session.

Years ago, fishing rivers like the Thames and Great Ouse, I would always take a variety of baits for roach. Apart from maggots, I would always have a pint each of hempseed and stewed wheat and possibly a tub of small worms. The hemp and wheat would invariably be used in preference to maggots, which would have a tendency to attract unwanted bleak. Bites with hemp would be lightning fast and a quick reaction was needed to connect with the roach but the bait would account for some good bags of fish. Wheat would often result in fewer but bigger fish; it had to be fed sparingly, as a few grains would soon satisfy a few decent roach – it is a filling meal.

Both hempseed and wheat are best prepared separately the day before by boiling the bait in water for half an hour and switching off the heat. By evening it would be fully cooked and drained through a sieve and transferred to a bait box. I still use hemp, not as bait but as a feed, especially with sweet corn, when I am roving in search of roach shoals or single big fish.

Tares are a bait I have rarely used for roach. They are certainly popular for roach in some parts of my region when used in conjunction with hemp and casters.

Worms, small ones that is, I have sometimes used for roach, but not with any conviction as they have a tendency to attract small perch. They are definitely favoured by the match angler for all species, as are bloodworms, which have always been a popular bait for roach.

Roach love a single grain of sweetcorn, especially taking it on the drop. I sometimes use it as bait in conjunction with corn and hemp fed regularly. It's also a great bait fished with a feeder. Ready-flavoured tins of corn can be bought in tackle shops or you can flavour or colour your own using products from the bakery section of supermarkets. I've used strawberry flavours on occasion, but I can't say that it proved to be any more successful than the natural product.

Elderberries were once a favourite bait of mine, I used to collect bunches of them when in season and preserve them in large jars for the remainder of the season. They were great fished with hemp and were especially useful where elderberry trees lined the riverbank.

I have never used pellets for roach, but the sheer volume of them used these days must have resulted in roach finding them irresistible. I guess the smaller the pellet used the more they will catch.

Combination baits are always worth a try: maggot/worm, corn/maggot, maggot/caster and so on. They will often work when one type of bait fished alone is ignored, and are often the first choice of bait for roach for some anglers.

Groundbait

Tackle shops will have a good stock of a variety of brands of groundbait. Most will serve their purpose, but I much prefer the basic white coarse breadcrumb which is less freely available nowadays. It can be made into anything from a cloud bait to a ball as hard as a peach, depending on the amount of water added.

To make a mix, put a little water into a bucket, add some breadcrumb and leave for ten minutes or so for the crumb to soak up the water, then stir up and continue to add more crumb for a stiffer mix. Bait samples can be added. Keep adding crumb if you want to make hard balls of groundbait.

If I am fishing bread, I add stale bread to water and add a little crumb and leave for a while, adding more crumb in stages to get the stiffness required.

With any groundbait, be it just hook-bait samples or a groundbait mix, too little is better than over feeding.

Fishing Styles
Stillwater techniques

I never use a pole, so I am not the person to give advice on them. Their efficacy is undeniable; it is that I just don't like to use them. If you wish to use one, articles frequently appear in the angling press which detail their usage, otherwise DVDs are available.

All the stillwaters I have fished respond to float fishing for roach. I do ledger for tench and sometimes catch unintended species, but not roach. That is not to say ledgering with a feeder is not successful for roach; it certainly can be but it is not a technique I employ, as I much prefer to float fish. There is

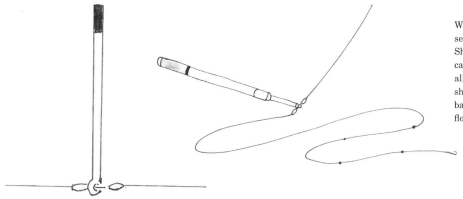

Waggler float rig – a very sensitive float-fishing method. Shot can be spaced out for catching on the drop and allowing the bait to drift. Bulk shot near the hook will hold the bait in place – bites will see the float rise in the water.

nothing complicated about my float fishing methods for roach. I use only three float types: a waggler, a drift beater and sometimes an onion-bodied float.

If the water is not too deep and relatively calm, I will use a waggler. The smaller the size the better, but if I am fishing at a distance or maybe the depth is greater, I would use a larger float. Any sort of waggler will do (I prefer the 'crystal' type), and any colour tip will do as long as it is bright orange!

Attaching the float depends on the type of eye it has. If the eye is a simple ring, I push a loop of line through it, pass the loop over the top of the float and gently tighten. To change the depth, push the loop

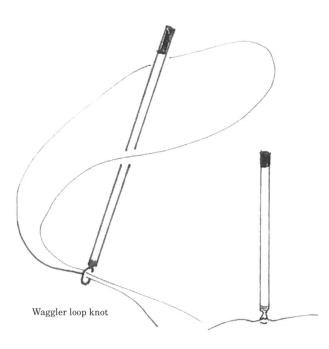

Waggler loop knot

again through the eye and adjust by pulling on one end of the loop.

If the eye of the float is too small or sharp-edged, avoid using this method and fix the float in place by pinching small shot either side of the float, or use float stops.

Shotting very much depends on the depth of the water and the float size. I generally fish a bait on the bottom, in which case I pinch the bottom shot, a BB or smaller, four to six inches from the hook when using a small waggler, otherwise, if the float is larger, I will have most of the shot near the hook. The closer the shot is to the bait, the more clearly it will register lift bites.

If bites are tentative, I will reduce the size of the bottom shot, even intentionally allowing the float to drift. That movement often induces a bite. Bites can vary from the float disappearing out of sight to lifting slightly. On one lake I fish, the depth is four to five feet, and the last time I fished there I had 48 nice roach, but the float never went under once –the bites were just a short lift of the waggler. I avoid the fine-tipped insert waggler floats; they are marginally more sensitive, but they're a strain on the eyes when you're watching them all day, especially in choppy water. That is a personal choice though. Straight wagglers can also be fished with a float cap near the top in tight swims, such as near lily pads.

Wagglers are fine for most situations, but for

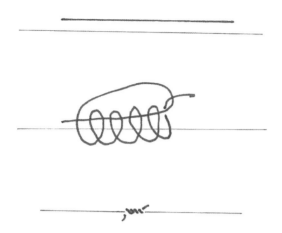

The stop knot. Use a heavier short length of line to tie the knot to give stiff ends, sufficient to stop the float passing over it.

choppy or deep water (over ten feet) I use a drift beater or onion-bodied float, usually the former.

I attach the drift beater in the same way as a waggler, that is, a loop through the eye if possible or with shot or float stops either side of the float eye. If the depth of water is too great to use a fixed float, I use the drift beater as a sliding float. To stop the float sliding too far up the line I use a stop knot – a knot I forgot to mention but essentially it is the same as a loop knot. To tie it, estimate on the line the depth of the water and importantly add roughly an extra three feet (it is something that can be experimented

with), then with a loop of thicker line (6-8lb) hold it against the line and make four or five turns around the main line with one end of the loop line, pull tight and trim off, sufficiently enough to stop the knot passing through the eye of the float. Also remember the stop knot will have to pass though the rod rings when casting, so it shouldn't be too tight as it might need moving.

All the shot except for one small one, say a no. 6, should be bulked a few inches from the hook, about four to six inches or as you wish. Use fractionally more shot than the float needs – it will help keep the float in place and stop it drifting. I usually use just a drilled bullet stopped by a micro bead, as described previously. The small shot should be three to four feet above the bulk shot; this is to avoid the float tangling around the bulk shot and bait when casting. Cast out and you will find the float slides up the line until it stops at the knot, and it should lie flat. Tighten the line and the float will stand upright. If it starts to drift, the bulk shotting needs to be increased. Just the tip of the float needs to be showing. Remember the baited hook will be slightly beyond the drift beater.

This is, of course, the lift method, and is ultra-sensitive. It is a terrific way to float fish and bites will be shown by the float dipping under or rising

Sliding drift beater float rig for deeper water. The stop knot should be three feet or more above the depth, bulk shot 4" – 6" from the hook and a small shot at least 3' – 4' above to stop tangles when casting

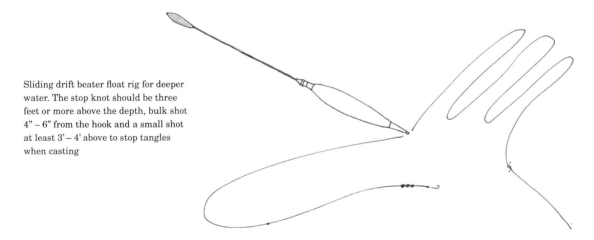

then lying flat – the time to strike. Strike on a rising float if you are alert enough.

I use onion-bodied floats occasionally in place of a waggler, probably in depths I can just manage with a fixed float. Fished like a waggler, they add a little more stability.

For roach, not a lot of groundbait is necessary. Just a few samples of hookbait fed regularly using a catapult. Likewise with a groundbait mix – feed little and often. The more frequent the bites, the more groundbait can be used. Catching the first fish is often critical; often the shoal is inactive, but hook a fish and its flashing and darting will often act as a trigger to get the shoal interested. So ring the changes to get that first bite, and try different baits, depths and parts of the swim. Twitching the bait along the bottom is often an inducement for a bite, as it is with any type of fishing.

Line strength is very much dependent on what other species are present. A two-pound line is fine if only roach are present, but if there are a few carp and tench about, a three or four-pound line is a better option. Otherwise a feeder can be used with a four to six-pound line.

Certainly if the target range is beyond twenty-five yards a feeder will be almost essential. An open ended or a maggot feeder will do, but avoid any that are fixed. If bites are not too frequent, two quiver rods can be used with different baits fished on each. A maggot or maggot/caster or worm cocktail on one rod with a size 16 hook and corn, a single kernel, or a small pellet on the other with a size 12 or 14 hook would be a good start.

On one of my local pits that I have fished in summer, I have caught tench, bream, carp, rudd and perch on the float and ledger but never a roach, yet one angler tells me he catches good roach at range in the evenings using casters with a feeder. On the adjacent pit I have caught roach after roach using bread at two rod lengths. Roach plainly don't play by the rules and can be extremely unpredictable, but start with the basics and in most cases you won't go wrong. I would rate maggots and bread flake as the two most successful baits on stillwaters, though pellets may be catching up on waters where they are fed in vast quantities.

Canal fishing for roach needs to be delicate; big carp may be present on some canals, but they are localised and it is best to assume that it will be mostly redfins present. A small to medium waggler will do in most cases and it's best to fish mainly on the bottom, shotting well up. Aiming to catch on the drop is well worth the effort. There is no need for heavy baiting, as just a few hook samples fed at intervals are often all that is necessary. Maggots, casters and seed baits work very well with samples fed with a 'pult little and often. Most canals are a joy to fish, especially rural ones, where you are likely to see few other anglers. Urban canals have their own attractions and can be productive and at times you can forget all about outlook when those redfins are biting.

Fenland drains can offer some great roach fishing too. Pike have been the target when I have fished them, but generally I've taken a few maggots along and often that has been enough to account for some good bags of prime roach. It's not incongruous that where you find there is good pike fishing there is also good roach fishing and vice versa. I was once fishing a narrow drain and a big roach leapt out of the water having been pursued by a pike. It landed on the far bank and remained there, still alive, for the remainder of the day. Perhaps it was waiting for nightfall, which wasn't far away, for a safe return to the water. My tackle for Fenland roach was a slim balsa float, probably one of my own making, shotted at intervals with a size 16 hook.

It is a peculiarity of canals and drains that

although the depth and width will be uniform for miles, some areas feel cold and soulless, yet a hundred yards further along the invariable bank, we stop and sense that this is the area to fish. A digestion of all the features we have observed, or a sixth sense?

River techniques

Roach fishing on rivers, to me, is all about trotting a float. Over 95 per cent of my river redfin fishing is carried out that way, and all the bigger roach I have caught have come using the float. I certainly would not like to restrict myself to one method for all my fishing, but trotting a float would be on my short list – a very short list. There is something special about watching a float meandering downstream in the current with the expectation of a bite at any second. Walk down any riverbank where an angler is trotting a float and you can't help but stop and follow its path. If it dips under, you mentally strike and wonder why the angler has taken so long to respond, but you can be forgiven for forgetting that the angler has not only

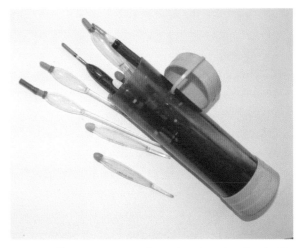

to mentally react as you have but has to physically strike with the rod as well.

The only time I don't float-fish for roach is when it is not the best option, which is when the river is high or in flood and the swim is confined.

I have spent many years river fishing for roach, from the River Colne in Middlesex, the Thames, the Great Ouse and the Hampshire Avon to the Medway, the Kennet, the Arun and the Suffolk, Kentish and Dorset Stours, and probably a few other rivers

An atmospheric sunset on one of my favourite Thames roach swims

besides. On most I have, at times, had some good bags of roach, especially from the Thames from Richmond to as far upstream as Buscot, but my pursuit of bigger fish has been almost entirely on the Hampshire Avon and to a much lesser extent the Dorset Stour.

Roach fishing on the Thames was great sport, and on most occasions I was rewarded with a good catch. The flow of the Thames is far from sedate in many places and my favourite swims were in places like Bourne End; there was a very good pace to the stream, even in autumn. The chosen swim at Bourne End was a good twenty yards long and I caught many a roach at the end of the trot. Bait was usually maggots or casters, a little fed with every trot down. The float would have been a slender balsa with a good-sized tip so that bites could be picked up at distance. The line strength was 3lb bs and the hook size a 14 or 16.

At Windsor, the flow was equally good. The roach there especially responded to hemp; a few grains were fed every cast and often an immediate bite followed as soon as the float settled. The length of the trot was no more than eight yards. The float, line and hook were the same, except that a size 16 hook was always used with a single grain of hempseed. I would have scaled down to a slightly lighter line, but barbel were present and I did hook and land some when I occasionally switched to maggots or casters.

Standard floats for slow or medium-paced flow, hand-made from balsa and cork. Stick floats are, of course, very popular and generally effective, but they are not for me. Some 'bites' are false (the bait/shot catching the bottom or weed) or a fish merely intercepting the bait; a stick float often won't differentiate between the two, but a longer tipped float will more likely tell you if the bite is false or 'animate'. The choice of float is, however, a matter of personal choice. Wagglers, if skilfully controlled, can be very effective.

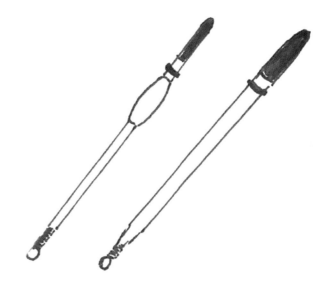

Hempseed was a bait I used to great effect on much of the Thames. Even when I was a schoolboy the Thames at Richmond was within cycling range, and I did have a few good roach on hemp there, but not in any great numbers; I habitually seem to arrive at the wrong state of the tide, having to fish on a rising tide – not the best time to catch.

Roach love to feed on hemp on the drop and in most cases bites will be almost instant and lightning quick. Watch redfins feeding on the seed and they will be darting about the swim looking for bait mid-depth yet ignoring grains littering the river bed. Fish 'laying on', that is with the float over depth and the hookbait on the bottom, and hemp can be less effective. This is where maggots, casters and bread can work, though hemp is still worth feeding to keep the shoal in the swim. Laying on is a great way to fish when bites are few and far between and will often account for a better stamp of fish. It's also a good method to fish for roach under overhanging trees, especially if they happen to be elderberry trees. Getting the amount of overdepth and rod tip to float distance can be problematic, but get it right and it can be a very enjoyable way to fish. The method is usually fished downstream, but I've seen some Thames roachers fish it upstream to perfection. Bait droppers, small ones, can be very useful when laying on.

Casting further afield

As young anglers age we kind of go along with the flow, which is probably a good thing. We are limited by vehicular mobility and funding as to where we can fish and what tackle is affordable. Local waters will be more familiar than distant ones and if we have an in-built desire to fish we will go home happy, whatever fish grace our net.

As we grow into adulthood and have a few more pounds in our pockets, and with good fortune own some sort of motor transport, our sights will be set upon waters further afield, where our aims will be set a step higher. It may well be, if we are lucky, that we already live near to a fine stretch of river or a marvellous lake, in which case the emphasis will be on improving our collection of tackle, be it rods and reels, bait, clothing or luggage. We can jump ahead of ourselves and miss out on what would be a progression of gradual improvement through a series of new experiences, each one memorable and a degree better than the last.

My own fishing, for roach in particular, had reached a point where, although I was enjoying every minute spent catching redfins from favourite swims on the River Thames, I considered my options. I had fished further afield, including the Hampshire Avon, where as a teenager the club coach visited each season, and apart from fishing the river a good number of times for barbel, I had had a few day trips by myself and with friends to float fish for roach and whatever else took my bait.

The Avon was in a different league, and there was a sense of adventure about fishing the quieter, more picturesque swims. The fame of the Avon was captivating. There was a chance of catching wonderful fish, but it was by no means easy; it was a challenge of ability and determination. The Thames offered consistency, but the Avon represented desire. The Avon won the contest, so I abandoned the Thames and became committed to the Avon for my river roach fishing.

My roaching would generally start after the first few frosty nights of autumn, when the weed growth was beginning to die off. A day on the river was still a long one, even in the winter months, for I would have tackled up before sunrise and fished through until after darkness fell. I was fishing new stretches, having joined the clubs in the Avon valley. The Salisbury & District Angling Club had some fine fisheries and most weekends I barely saw another angler on the bank. Perhaps I had missed the peak of the Avon roaching, for I never had the great bags of redfins that had been caught in earlier years, but I did have a few good fish and generally I would catch on most trips.

If I failed to catch a roach, at least I would have caught other species: dace, grayling, perch, chub, trout and the odd salmon. Once that float dipped under the surface I simply never knew what I was going to hook. Dace would put up a spirited fight, trout would dash about leaping out the water, a solid resistance would be felt whenever a salmon was hooked followed by a series of powerful runs, but it was the jagged fight that I was hopeful of – that would signify a roach. I can never forget the elation of catching my first two-pound roach and a few more that followed up to two and a quarter pounds – truly magnificent specimens. Later, having made the house move to be near the Avon, I was able to spend more time fishing for roach (and barbel) with greater intensity, and trying new venues, eventually being rewarded with some very good fish.

One wonders what the roach fishing on the Avon must have been like in bygone days. I don't think it was always easy, but when things went right

My long-term friend George Morris of Fordingbridge has caught not only fine barbel but some super roach to 3lb 3oz. This Avon redfin weighed 2lb 4oz.

some outstanding catches were made. Recalling some of the writings in my older books, catches of a hundredweight (over 50kg) of roach were possible, and I remember an account of two guys fishing in a punt on what they thought was not a favourable day. Their day's catch included seven perch over two pounds, the largest three pounds, dace up to fifteen ounces, two grayling, one of them two and a quarter pounds, and 167 roach, nineteen of which were over two pounds, the best two and three quarters. They would have done better were it not for the pike in the swim! Dob Chislett of Christchurch Angling Club wrote about roach fishing on the Avon and once recounted a match he fished on the lower river. From memory he had eighty pounds plus of roach and only came seventh or eighth in the match!

My best day on the Avon did result in over a hundred pounds of fish; some were roach but only ten over a pound. The rest were 22 chub, seven barbel, 60 dace and a pound and a half perch, plus another that might have been three pounds, lost at the net. The following day I caught one two-ounce dace, the day after that an eighty-pound catch. Needless to say I had fished different swims on the three days.

I have never caught more than two 2lb roach in a day's fishing, but I couldn't have been happier with that catch. A 2lb roach is a super fish and I have been delighted whenever I have caught one. Some very good roach anglers may not have caught a two pounder; it is no reflection on their ability to catch bigger redfins, it's simply that fish of two pounds probably don't exist in the waters they fish.

The place where I caught my first two-pound roach on the Avon was electro-fished a number of years later and I understand not a single roach was found. There is no doubt that it suffered a decline. In my opinion, I can only repeat that it is the result of the pernicious, savage weedcutting that was carried out for many years, added to which has been the predation by cormorants and the influence of effluent from trout farms.

Roach fishing on the Avon is still worth the effort. They may not be as widespread as they once were and there are probably fewer big fish than before, but there are signs that the fishing is improving on some stretches, with weed growth returning to what it once was. Clubs will give details of fish stocks on their waters and where best to catch that magical two-pounder. All you have to do is catch one. Good luck.

I have to give credit once more to the Avon Roach Project, which is doing great work in breeding redfins and restocking the river. Their work can be viewed on the Avon Roach Project website and I understand similar ventures have started up elsewhere on other rivers. Credit also to the Environment Agency, which has helped with the project. Donations to the Avon Roach Project will greatly help with their work.

I have deviated somewhat from my details on river float techniques, but I've wanted to give an insight into how my conviction to Avon roaching came about and how my tackle choice and technique has changed in line with how I fished the river initially and how I approach the river today. I have to disagree with early writings on the Avon, blaming the inadequacy of the visiting angler's tackle and the inability to fish the fast-flowing water because of its intimidating nature. Sure, you might need a slightly larger float with extra shot, but that is about it. Fast-flowing rivers abound throughout the land and I'm sure any angler competent at fishing their local river will have no trouble coping with the Avon after a couple of sessions.

It was common for the Avon float angler to use lines up to 4lb for roach and I may well have done so initially myself. Hook sizes were larger too. A little more finesse is required these days if you've any chance of success.

My float choice on the Avon was always the fluted type; made of balsa, they were compact, took enough shot and were very stable in following the course of the current.

Fluted floats have a central stem with four vanes running most of the length. How they were made I don't know, but they were beautifully crafted and fortunately I still have some. Quite possibly they are still available from specialist float makers or angling memorabilia dealers.

As it happened my roach swims were not too deep – four to five feet, six at the most. The Avon is generally not a deep river; the one deep stretch that springs to mind has been dredged in the not too distant past. There may well be deep holes throughout the river, but I've never associated them with roach.

Shotting was generally shirt-button style, BB or AAA spaced eight inches or more apart with a small shot loosely pinched below the float, once the required depth was found. The bottom shot depended upon the bait used; a small shot for maggots and at least a BB shot for bread. Both maggots and bread were used for bait and more often than not a breadcrumb groundbait, especially when using bread as bait. Bread accounted for the bigger roach but far fewer fish.

Maggots were more commonly used, with anything up to a gallon used in a day. Wading in the shallows, maggots could be fed by hand, using a maggot pouch around the neck or a bait apron around the waist, otherwise a catapult was the best way of feeding further afield. Bread, a piece of flake on a size

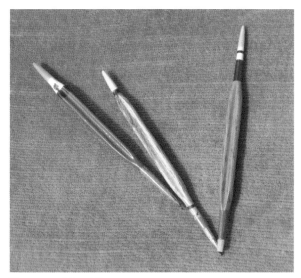
My treasured fluted floats

12 or 10 hook, would be used with groundbait. The rig would be the same for both baits except for hook size and the bottom shot; when using bread a larger shot would be used to keep the hookbait nearer the bottom.

Although bread accounted for the better roach, maggots would always produce more bites, and not only from roach. Rainbow trout, in particular, had a penchant for the wriggly chaps, often coughing up numbers of the freebies the swim had been fed with.

I continued to fish for roach on the Avon over successive years, but sometimes there were interruptions for pike and an increasing interest in barbel during the winter months. Then, living near the Avon, I had good roach fishing on my doorstep and began fishing for redfins in earnest. Indeed, my local stretch began to turn up some huge roach, the biggest an outstanding three pounds ten ounces, but the publicity soon began to attract a great deal of attention. I had no trouble in identifying the location of captures in the press; the backgrounds in the pictures were easily recognisable.

My interests were elsewhere, in places where the banks were often deserted and well away from the madding crowd. My tackle had changed little. I still used the same fixed-spool reel but with a new rod, and the target was big roach or nothing. So it was bread flake almost solely for bait and stale bread and crumb for groundbait. The line strength was reduced to two and half pounds, even two pounds at times. The standard hook was a Drennan size 12 Specimen.

I've already mentioned the maggot/bread difference, but it's more than just the bait in question, it's the mindset that needs to be explained. Fishing bread can be very frustrating; bites will be few and far between, and the day may well be a blank one. You return home tired after a fruitless session, return the next day and another blank follows and quite possibly the same happens again and again, but then one day things go well and you'll be rewarded with that prize redfin. Roach fishing with bread is like that; you just need patience. I say blanks, but chub are abundant on the Avon at present and you will likely catch a few before the roach feed.

On the new venues I was fishing, the roach

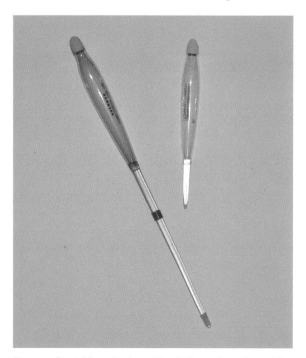
Drennan Crystal Long Loafer and Loafer floats: these along with Crystal Avons are ideal for most of my river fishing

swims were somewhat deeper than those I had fished previously, being more often over six feet than under. This called for a more buoyant float, and I began to try the Drennan Crystal Avons, which had been on the market for a little while. They proved perfect for the swims I wanted to fish, the only minor criticism being that the tip could have been a fraction longer. I changed my shot pattern to bulk shotting, set at a depth according to the flow. The greater the flow the nearer the bulk shot should be to the bait. Mostly now I use a 2.5lb main line and about a 15-18in 2lb hook length, with the shot always above the adjoining knot. On occasions I have used 2lb line straight through to the hook, when the going gets tough, as it often does. In apparently perfect conditions, the day can be biteless. It is hard work trotting a float for hours on end and enervating at the end of the session. At times I have said to myself after a blank day that I will give it a miss on the morrow and even felt the same the next morning, only to find myself back on the riverbank after lunch. The compulsion to fish is omnipotent. Perhaps today will be the day the big roach decide to feed and there is always the magnetism of being in such marvellous surroundings, which in itself is enough to draw me back.

Again, I still use a small shot just below the float to stop it slipping. I slightly under-shot the float to begin with until I get the depth right, then add the final shot under the float.

I gave a lot of thought to the significance of the shot nearest the hook. What should the distance be? Baiting with bread, I inevitably drop bits of flake and crust at my feet, which I pick up at the end of the day and put in my groundbait bucket. The following day they will be soggy, and stirred in with the remaining crumb left in the bucket they will act as good freebies when baiting the swim. I want my hookbait to behave the same as the freebies, naturally fluttering and dancing in the flow, not behaving like a ball in a skittle alley. So that is how I came to the conclusion that the minimum hook-to-shot distance should be fifteen to eighteen inches.

Using the bulk shot slightly below mid depth in normal flow I use just one shot, probably a BB, fifteen to eighteen inches above the hook, plus, of course, the shot below the float. I don't measure the distance each time, I merely pinch the bottom shot at a distance that feels about right. If I have the bulk shot near the hook, I pinch one or two small shot mid-depth to avoid too much of a bow in the line below the float.

I found it interesting to read later on that the great roacher Captain Parker had come to the same conclusion in his book *This Fishing*; he advocated never having shot nearer than eighteen inches from the hook, regardless of bait. I wouldn't go so far as to say that was right for all baits, especially hemp, maggots and casters, and occasionally the swim might be shallow enough to warrant moving the bottom shot nearer the hook to keep the bait closer to the river bed.

Earlier I mentioned two useful accessory items, Plasticine or modelling clay and float cap tubing. Shot, especially if used bulked, hardly looks natural. To mitigate the unnatural appearance I use Plasticine (and I'm sure modelling clay would work as well) to cover it. Just a small pinch of the softened material can be moulded around the shot to form an elongated shape; a flattened pinch the size of a 20p coin will suffice and will barely add any weight. Provision for it can be made anyway by marginally reducing one of the shot sizes. The resulting shape will more likely resemble something vegetative in the current. I use brown, but brown or green, the colour probably doesn't matter too much, I don't think. It does have a tendency to begin to break open after continued retrieval of the float, about every thirty minutes or so, but is squeezed back into shape within seconds.

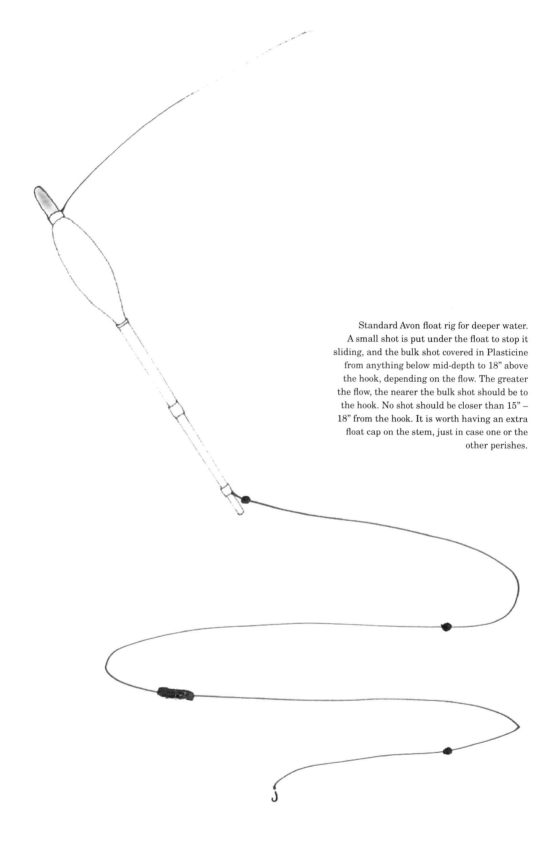

Standard Avon float rig for deeper water. A small shot is put under the float to stop it sliding, and the bulk shot covered in Plasticine from anything below mid-depth to 18" above the hook, depending on the flow. The greater the flow, the nearer the bulk shot should be to the hook. No shot should be closer than 15" – 18" from the hook. It is worth having an extra float cap on the stem, just in case one or the other perishes.

The material can be reused and a block will last countless years.

Float tubing will serve three purposes: firstly, the obvious, is to snip off short lengths to replace perished or broken float caps. The second is to act as a dark float tip in fading light conditions; a length of about an inch and a half (40mm) is about right. Dark colours are best; I find dark blue is the best choice. It is much easier seeing a dark-coloured tip in the half-light of dusk, especially when looking towards the western horizon. It might only give fifteen to twenty minutes at most of extra fishing time, but that may prove time enough to catch a good roach or two. Mates returning to the car park have said to me that I can't possibly be seeing the float anymore, but I can, and that's why.

The third application of tubing is again to use as a sight, but this time in rough water which is being whipped up by the wind. The surface on exposed, windy areas can be very choppy and it can be very difficult following the float tip down the swim. If the wind gets up I use two inches (50mm), maybe even three inches if necessary of tubing on the float

Bulk shot covered with a small pinch of green or brown Plasticine – every tactic helps with big, wily roach.

tip, and again blue is best. It's amazing how highly visible it is – and even more amazing to watch it sail out of sight! Ostensibly I can be trotting a float, which otherwise would be invisible most of the time. The tubing does cause the float to waver about on the retrieve, which is best avoided by holding the rod tip higher and winding in quicker.

There is the odd, very rare, occasion when I don't use an Avon float with bread, and that is when the river is running high and fast and boiling, in which case I use a big Drennan Loafer, carrying at least three SSG shot, which I use in the same way as an Avon. Loafers are very buoyant and stable in fast currents and the small ones are ideal for fishing shallower swims. Obviously the bait needs to get to the bottom as quickly as possible and the shot will need to be closer to the hook.

Recently I have been looking at carp waggler floats, and wondering if they would make good floats in heavy water; they certainly take plenty of shot, three SSG and above, and have high-visibility vaned tips. I've yet to try one.

I have yet to mention hand-made floats, which are beautifully crafted and can be works of art. I have one or two fragile examples, but I've been too frightened to use them for fear of breakage. More robust models are made and although not cheap, they should last for years and would be joyful to use. I quite fancy getting a few, solely for display.

Although I use bread almost exclusively for roach on the Avon, there is the odd occasion when I might use maggots, and as it happens, on my last session I did use some. I had been looking at a very narrow side stream, which was totally overgrown; I'm not even sure who it belongs to. In one or two places I saw some good roach, some certainly over two pounds. Back at the car I bumped into a friend who was going home after a morning's fishing and he gave me a pint of maggots which he had no further use for. I gratefully accepted them and thought I

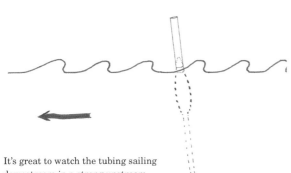

It's great to watch the tubing sailing downstream in a strong upstream wind – even greater when it disappears

would look for somewhere to drop a float into the side stream; there was a short channel less than three feet deep, which I could trot a small loafer down, so I gave it a try. Feeding maggots by hand and baiting a size 16 hook with a single maggot, I instantly started catching roach, superb, plump fish, some over the pound mark, and wondered if they had ever been caught before. After a short session I had three dozen prime roach, and I would have caught more had it not been for a greedy jack pike.

Fishing in such a small, shallow swim I needed to get the bait down quickly so I spread the small shot evenly over a couple of feet, the nearest to the hook was six inches. Not a case for having an eighteen inch gap between the hook and first shot.

Generally when I fish maggots it is for grayling, which I do when the mercury falls below zero, but I often catch some good roach in the process. I use a lighter Avon float and spread the shot evenly to within eight or ten inches of the hook.

With bread, I pinch a fingernail piece of flake from a fresh white loaf onto the top of the hook shank with the point exposed. The soft part of the bread is on the side opposite the hook bend. Others attach their bread in different ways and it probably doesn't matter a great deal, as long as the hook point is slightly exposed.

On arrival, I feed two or three kiwi-sized (the fruit, not the All Black rugby player) balls of groundbait if the swim is familiar to me. If the swim

Trotting in floodwater

is a new one I will trot the float down first to see if it is free of weed or snags. There's no point in baiting a swim you're not going to fish, it's just wasting bait. Once settled in a swim, I feed one ball every five out of six trots down, the idea being that fish might be accustomed to the frequency of feed and on one cast the one freebie on offer might be the one on my hook!

I look for different types of bites. Naturally there is the one where the float dives under, which is unmistakable, but other bites can be subtle. A float will dip and bounce as it travels downstream as a consequence of the undulations of the river bottom and weed beds, but I look for when the float dips, then dips further, or when it bounces a little more than it would do normally; both can be delicate deviations but will signify a bite. Stopping the float at the end of the swim and holding it still for a few seconds will cause the bait to rise and flutter in the current, and often this will induce a bite – a dipping of the float or a tightening of the line. Often the only bites of the day are during those few seconds of stoppage. Also, be alert to bites on the drop, which are more frequent than would be expected.

Trotting a float properly comes with practice. Both fixed-spool reels and centre-pins are okay, but my choice nowadays is always a centre-pin, as they

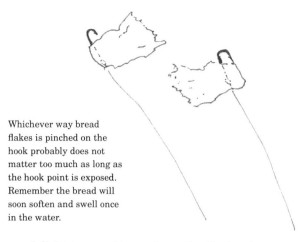

Whichever way bread flakes is pinched on the hook probably does not matter too much as long as the hook point is exposed. Remember the bread will soon soften and swell once in the water.

are a delight to use. Always keep the float a degree under control, and moving slightly more slowly than it would on its own; never leave a fixed-spool bail arm open without any control. Remember the flow on the river bed is slower than it is on the surface.

With a fixed-spool reel the technique is to release a few yards of line at a time off the spool under control, using your finger on the spool, at the same time raising the rod tip, keeping the line tight to the float, then lowering the rod tip to allow the float to continue on its course and repeating the action until the float reaches the end of the swim. The bail arm can then be closed, then wait for a few seconds for that end-of-swim bite. All very basic stuff and not too difficult to perform, just that the float should be kept under control all the time and a bite should be anticipated at any time.

There is nothing complicated about using a

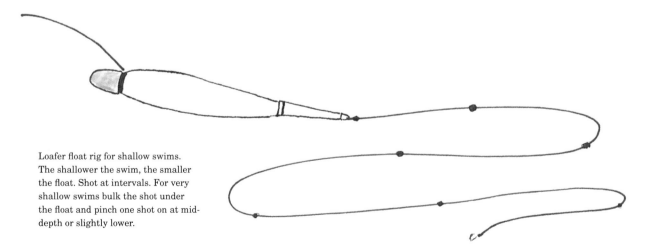

Loafer float rig for shallow swims. The shallower the swim, the smaller the float. Shot at intervals. For very shallow swims bulk the shot under the float and pinch one shot on at mid-depth or slightly lower.

Trotting on an Avon swim

centre-pin; simply cast and keep control of the turn of the drum with the thumb of the hand on the rod. If the reel doesn't spin enough from the pull of the float, it is not up to it and needs cleaning and oiling. All centre-pins need a drop of oil on the spindle occasionally. A flick of the thumb on the drum might help if the flow is slow and the float small, but if that still doesn't work, the reel isn't free-running enough and might need upgrading. Again, trotting with a centre-pin is not that difficult once mastered and it is truly a terrific way to fish.

I sometimes fish the Dorset Stour, maybe for barbel or chub, but often in the summer months roach grab my attention. The river is clear and often fish can be seen. On occasion barbel, chub, dace and roach may be in the same swim and it is the roach that I will fish for, which can be large but very wily.

Whether it is roach in a shoal of mixed species or sole big roach that I have spotted whilst roving, the tactic will be much the same. I will feed the swim by hand with a mixture of hemp and sweetcorn, little

Use your thumb for rim control of a centre-pin

and often, and fish a grain of corn on a size 14 hook with a float. The float will be a small loafer with about three shot on the line, the bottom shot twelve inches from the hook. roach like to take the loose feed on the drop and I aim to catch fish in the same manner. It is a difficult but great way to catch roach, something I ought to do more of but finding the big redfins is not easy.

I vividly remember fellow Barbel Catchers' Club member Mike Lamb taking me to the Stour, where

Dorset Stour roach – small or not so small?

Ian May with a 3lb roach, caught ledgering upstream

he had caught and spotted some big roach. There were indeed roach in his tight swim, some smaller ones and some about a pound, I estimated. I fed hemp and corn as Mike lowered his corn bait into the five-foot-plus swim. Eventually one of the 'pound' fish visibly took the corn bait and Mike hooked the roach, and as it came up towards the surface in the confined swim, it got bigger and bigger. Safely landed, it was weighed and the scales registered about two and a half pounds. Another followed shortly after, of similar weight. I just wonder how big some of the roach I have seen over the years have been.

Painted alignment dots on quiver rods aid quick assembly

Ledgering on Rivers

There is not a great deal of difference between ledgering on a river and stillwater ledgering, except that in most cases an underarm cast will suffice to reach most spots. The same rods, reels, lines and hooks can be used and I favour bread flake as the best bait.

One or two light eleven-foot rods are ideal, with built-in quiver tips. Fixed-spool reels are preferable, loaded with no more than 4lb line. Hook size for bread would be a size 12 and for maggots and casters a size 16 or 14.

Pieces of bread flake very lightly pinched onto the link ledger will soon break off and drift temptingly downstream. A slightly heavier weight might be necessary using this ploy.

Quiver rod isotopes for night fishing

A perfect slack water swim for quiver tipping

127

There is no doubting the success of feeders, and for bread I would use a small caged type, not putting groundbait in the feeder but a few pinches of bread flake lightly squeezed so they will quickly be released on the river bed. A feeder is best attached on a link with a small bead used as a stop. Eighteen inches would be a good starting distance for the feeder to hook length. I rarely do use a feeder for roach though, much preferring a small Arlesey bomb on a running link.

For groundbait I use the same mix as for float fishing, stale bread and breadcrumb. I err on the side of less is best, considering there will likely be only a few roach in the swim. Just the odd egg-sized ball of groundbait fed every ten minutes should be enough. One trick I employ with only an Arlesey weight is to lightly pinch a couple of pieces of flake onto the ledger link, which will hopefully soon free themselves once on the bottom and settle close to the hookbait or trickle temptingly downstream. If there are any pieces still left on the retrieve, then they have been pinched on too tightly. To my knowledge, I have not had a roach grab a piece of flake on the link in preference to my hookbait.

Dusk and the first hour of darkness are always a good time for roach, and for bite indication I have isotopes whipped onto my quivers. Bites are usually unmistakable. Touch ledgering is better if using just one rod, and as I usually fish for roach in the winter, I keep my hands warm with fingerless thermal gloves.

Quiver-tipping is a super way to fish for roach on tree-lined banks when the river is swollen. Roach, in my experience, do not like slack water and I like to fish just into the flow where there is a crease between fast and slack water. The method has accounted for some great roach; the best I have seen weighed three pounds plus and was caught light ledgering upstream when the river was high.

Travelling light on a fine winter's day, it is a great way to unwind on the riverbank.

The enchanting Mill House at Breamore. Ringwood and DAC have extensive fishing downstream. Persevere for big roach and barbel.

The lower end of Fordingbridge Recreation Ground on the Hampshire Avon – historically a great roach water

One of the Rec's good trotting swims

Britford, south of Salisbury. Miles of riverbank and top-rated for roach. Shoals can be localised – seek the river keeper for helpful advice.

End of season on the Dorset Stour at Christchurch Quay. Great trotting water on the ebb tide.

The top water on the Royalty in summer and winter – scene of some big roach captures.

Where to fish for roach

Roach can be found in most rivers and stillwaters, but a little local knowledge is always a great help. A local tackle shop is the best first port of call; advice will be given on the best local waters and how to get a ticket or how to join a club in the area. Club sites will detail their fisheries and fish stocks. Magazines are also a good source of information on where to fish.

A few years ago I had the pleasure of photographing and sometimes doing the write-ups for venues in my area for the *Anglers' Mail* 'Where to Fish' series. The aim of the series is to give an accurate description of the fishery, with details on fish stocks and size, how best to fish, how to obtain a ticket and how to get there. The venue guide is a popular section of the magazine and I understand many anglers cut out the pages relating to their area and make a folder of them. There is a similar guide in *Angling Times*.

Clubs list their own 'best fish' records, which are a good pointer to where to find big roach. These captures may well have been a few years ago and that generation of big fish may have passed on, but some areas do have a pedigree for producing specimen fish decade after decade. Roach, like barbel, do travel but often have a 'home' swim. Perhaps their descendants have the same genes, which would explain the consistent presence of big fish in certain areas.

Yet roach fishing is not all about catching big fish – any day with a few redfins landed will be a good day. Catching roach of any size is enjoyable and fun, wherever you fish.

There used to be 'Where to Fish' books on the market, but they may no longer be in print. If you can get a copy of an old edition, they do make interesting reading. There are a number of websites that list fisheries county by county, as well as tackle shops and accommodation in the area.

Diary dates

I've always been a great one for keeping records, and my diaries list all my fishing sessions except for most of my teenage years. There are literally thousands of entries listed of days fished. Some entries may represent week-long sessions, but additionally there are hundreds, if not thousands, of mostly unrecorded days spent by the water, cheerfully roaming, intensively observing and assessing every vision and taking in the glorious environment. Time by the waterside breathes new life into me.

Every diary entry, apart from the early ones, shows the date and where I have fished, even if the day has been a fruitless one. But 'fruitless' is not the word, for I will have enjoyed the day, learning from the experience and finding the art of angling a delight as always. Looking at many of the entries, I don't recall what happened on the day, unless it was an eventful one, but each time I would have reflected on the day with a great deal of thought. Naturally some days will be highly memorable, mostly because they have been successful ones and I hardly need to refer to what I wrote about the occasion.

Two of those days I will recount in detail, from my diary and from memory.

Date: 11th March. I'd been fishing mainly for roach since the start of the year, taking a couple of days out for barbel and fortunately catching a couple of 'whiskers' and two chub. One day I caught several roach, the smallest around the pound mark, a number around the pound and a half mark and an amazing fish nudging three pounds, plus one dace. On two days I caught two 3lb chub and a 1lb roach. All my other sessions had been blanks. Most of my efforts were concentrated on one swim, which was one of my favourites for roach, yet I had failed to get a single bite so far.

I had fished the swim the previous year and never had one fish despite my efforts. I persisted in the swim because it looked perfect; I had previously

parted the tall, dead reeds just wide enough to create a space to fish from and a few yards downstream there was a small gap where I could land a fish. I always placed my landing net there in readiness on arrival. The width and depth of the length of river were fairly uniform, the level now was slightly above normal and I set my float at nearly six feet. There was a little weed still in the swim, but I knew where it was and had no trouble negotiating the float through it.

It was a fine day, with just a tinge to the water and it was terrific to be by the river. I had fished the swim two days earlier and the day before that without a bite, but I'm always optimistic. My diary tells me that on the 11th I arrived at one in the afternoon, the wind direction was from the south west and the weather was mild and bright. Tackle, as usual, was my 13ft Shimano and a small fixed-spool reel; I had dropped the line strength to 2lb as I knew the swim well by now. A size 12 hook was directly tied onto the line. The float was a Drennan Crystal Avon, with the shot bulked a fraction below mid depth with a BB shot fifteen or sixteen inches above the hook. I still had some groundbait left in the bucket, kept cool since my last visit, which allowed me to bait

and fish straight away. I dropped a couple of balls of groundbait in with an underarm swing and my float was on its way downstream, firstly working its way through some strands of weed – I knew exactly where they were – then trundling off and dragging the bread bait along the clean gravel river bed.

An hour or more passed without a bite, and then along came that fine roacher Ron Smith, whom I regard as a chum. Ron was actually on the far bank and another angler was fishing fifty yards or so below where he had settled. I waved to Ron, trying to avoid shouting across the river. As it was near to the end of the season there were a few more anglers on the bank, and upstream of me, a good hundred yards away, was a group of three fishing the same area.

Half an hour or so later, I noticed Ron striking and saw that he was into a fish. Three or four minutes passed and I could see it was a big roach, which he safely netted. From the smile on his face as he weighed the fish, I guessed how big it was. He called across to confirm it was a three-pounder – not Ron's first three, nor his last.

After an interval, I saw one of the anglers upstream also bringing a good fish to the net and wondered how big it was.

I fished on, still confident, and eventually got a bite. The float had barely settled when it slid away at an angle, a gentle strike and I was into a fish... could it be? After carefully playing it for a few minutes it came to the surface; it had red fins and it was big. Thankfully it was soon in the waiting net and I found myself gazing at a probable three-pound roach. The needle on the scales passed three pounds and stopped at almost half an ounce over, so I decided to settle for three pounds and a quarter ounce. Wow!

One of the upstream anglers wasn't too far away at the time and I asked if he could take a couple of photos, which he gladly did. He told me that the other fish caught had weighed three pounds six ounces!

My diary tells me that I caught the roach at 17:20, it was still light, and I fished on.

These big Avon roach are so rarely caught that three fish over the magical 3lb mark caught in one day from different spots was amazing, but unbelievably another roach was caught by the angler fishing below Ron which weighed two pounds twelve ounces. The four roach in total weighed over twelve pounds.

My diary also tells me I caught another fish, a chub of about three pounds, which I caught at the tail of the swim. Pity it wasn't another roach!

Date: 10th March. I had to check my diary for this next notable date; it was almost a year later, again in the last week of the season. The start of the year was a little colder and I noted an air temperature of zero in February. I fished around, catching some barbel from the Royalty, trout and grayling from the River Test and a few chub here and there. March was a little milder but windy, and I decided to spend the end of the season for roach. It was a time of opportunism, electing to fish where weather conditions dictated the best option, but I felt a compulsion to catch a good redfin from somewhere.

The river conditions were not good. The river had been in flood and now it was just within its banks, but with all the hatches open it was running off very fast and still coloured. Not the best time to fish, but as long as there's a bait in the water, there is always a chance.

I had one or two swims in mind; this was a case of having walked the banks in the clear conditions of summer and autumn paying dividends. One swim in particular had a large bed of 'cabbages' in the summer, which created a small but clean bed of fine gravel below. Now, in wintry conditions, the surface barely revealed the presence of the haven and it had to be my first choice of swim. It would have made a good barbel swim, but today I had my roach hat on.

Once more I arrived at my chosen spot at one in the afternoon. It looked like I had the river to myself, but no, incredibly Sylvester came walking along the bank soon after I began to arrange my tackle. I was beginning to think he had a doppelganger; I seemed to bump into him everywhere I fished. We're good chums though, and as usual we had a good chat about fishing. He was a bit downcast, having already fished my swim and others without a bite.

I started fishing around two o'clock, and somehow I still felt optimistic. Despite the fast flow, the water temperature was a favourable 9 degrees (49°, in old money). My tackle was 2.5lb line straight through with the biggest Crystal Avon I could find in my float tube. All the bulk shot was pinched on fifteen inches from the hook and covered with a small film of Plasticine. I wanted to get my bait quickly down into the hollow below the remains of the cabbages, where, hopefully there might be a roach or two. Minimal groundbait was required as I wished to get just a little to the bottom of the short swim, and doubtless Sylvester had put some in earlier.

The cast was just a gentle underarm swing to land the float two rod lengths out. I had to get it spot on, in exactly the position I wanted; fifteen inches too far upstream and the float would lie flat and slowly sink, having been caught on the cabbages. Fifteen inches too far downstream and the weight would have been out of the hollow and racing away with the current. I wouldn't have been surprised if there was a back-flow on the river bed created by the barrier of the cabbages. It was that critical, but once I got it right, I could then control the float, holding it back a fraction.

I fished on, and over two hours passed before I got my first bite. My record shows that it was twenty past four; I thought it had been earlier, but time passes quickly on a pleasant winter's afternoon session. The float zonked under; I can still remember the emphatic bite now. I struck and was instantly into a good fish and it chugged about in the swim, which was probably its living room. I wanted to get it on the front lawn. A few anxious minutes passed and I felt the fish rising to the surface, where it lay on its side for a couple of seconds. The bright red fins of the big fish told me what I had hoped for, it was a big roach.

I gently brought it into the big landing net and lifted it out of the water. I must have had a smile on my face, for it looked bigger than my previous three-pounder, though it didn't have the same metallic blue on its flanks; it looked more the colour of a pound roach, only three times as big. On the scales it weighed a good 3lb 1oz. Sylvester had seen me land the roach and witnessed the weighing. He took a couple of quick snaps with my camera and I returned the redfin to its home; it swam away back into the depths.

I did fish on until seven in the evening and I did catch another fish; by coincidence it was a chub again, which came from the tail of the swim. It weighed 4lb 1oz. Pity it wasn't a roach!

DIGBY CALLS

The next roach fishing tale goes back a few years to a fine August day. I was fishing on the Dorset Stour; it was my third visit to the swim, which was magnificent. I had yet to catch a fish or see one in the swim, which showed no signs of having been fished, no doubt because of its inaccessibility.

The spot had everything: varying depths, clean golden gravel beds, various abundant weed beds and plenty of bankside vegetation, as well as overhanging trees. Surely barbel wouldn't be far away, and there was every likelihood of big roach appearing from anywhere. Barbel were really the target, but I regularly sprinkled small offerings of hemp and sweetcorn with my catapult onto the open gravel patch in the centre of the swim in the hope of attracting roach. I had already baited the spot with the two baits using a bait dropper and I fished two grains of sweetcorn on a hair rig. The other bait, a cube of luncheon meat, was fished on a dark gravel area between two beds of bulrushes.

It was a speculative session, just to see if I could either catch a fish or observe any fish which made an appearance. I had no doubt whatsoever that there would be good fish in the area; it was just a case of getting to know the swim, and if I could manage several visits I was certain big fish would turn up at some time. The more bait I could put in on a regular basis, the greater the chance of fish homing in to feed.

I didn't fish till late, just to the point when I could no longer clearly see the river bed. It was all about surveillance. I never had a bite, but that mattered not.

I drove straight home, parked the car in the garage and began to prepare some food for a late dinner. I was about to put the meal on a plate when the phone rang, as it always tends to do at such times. I didn't instantly recognise the voice on the line but the name registered straight away. It was Digby, someone I have bumped into in the past on the River Avon, and we have chatted about roach, his one and only fishing passion. Digby was from Cheshire and was able to get down to Hampshire less frequently than he liked, but said he would be down the day after tomorrow. He wondered if I could point him in the direction of a good trotting swim on the Avon, where he was keen to try out his new cane rod. I explained that roach fishing on the Avon was difficult in the summer – good trotting swims were few and far between because of the weed growth and that the best bet was to try roving on the Stour, looking for fish. That didn't appeal to Digby. He said he didn't mind where he fished on the Avon as long as he could watch a float in the current and hopefully catch a fish or two. There was a local wooded stretch where he could probably catch a few fish, but I didn't think that was for him. There was a swim I knew further upstream that was always productive and I knew he could fish it as he had a club book that gave him access. The only problem was that it was by far the best trotting swim on the venue, so it was popular, and I really couldn't think of a plan B should the swim be occupied. Digby was fine with that and said he'd pick me up in his car in two days' time. I advised him to bring his waders and a good quantity of maggots as well as a few casters and some bread for bait.

Two days later I had only just finished breakfast when the doorbell rang, it was Digby. I apologised for not being quite ready and said that I would be out in a couple of minutes once had I fetched my bag, waders and coat from the garage. The car outside was a large black Mercedes estate and I asked Digby what the letters 'AMG' on the back stood for. 'Aufrecht Melcher Grossaspach,' Digby told me, but I knew roughly what it meant anyway – the high-performance arm of Mercedes. Digby had a driver, and he helped me put my stuff in the boot; his name was Sam, a short, stout guy, taciturn but polite. Whether it was a hire car or belonged to Digby, I didn't ask.

Digby was keen to know more about the swim, which I briefly described, but reiterated my concerns that it could well be occupied. He just seemed to be happy to be on his way to the river.

We shortly arrived at the car park, where there were already two cars. Sam unloaded the Merc and we donned our waders and put on our coats. Sam didn't have to be asked to carry Digby's gear, but he had to leave it when we reached the stile where the club-owned fishery began. The fishery wasn't familiar

to my guest, so I led the way on the ten-minute walk to the intended swim, still anxious whether or not it would be vacant. We had to negotiate a couple of ditches and cross rough ground which obscured the sight of the river. Would the swim be free? We soon found out – luckily, it was. What a relief. It was indeed a terrific swim to trot a float, and I think that was all that mattered to Digby.

A few yards back from the river's edge Digby began to hastily assemble his tackle and I couldn't help but notice his superb new cane rod, which still had a fine dusting of new cork on the handle. At a fraction short of twelve feet it was perfect for the swim and this would be the first time it would cast a float. The maker's name on the butt told me it must have cost a pretty penny. His small fixed-spool reel loaded with line of about two and a quarter pound bs was fine, but all his floats looked a little too large for the swim. I offered him the use of one of my slim balsa floats of about six inches, which would be ideal.

The swim was about four feet at the deepest and I suggested setting the float at four feet six inches to start with. Digby tied on a size 16 hook and I pinched on the shot for him. From memory it was a no. 1 eight inches above the hook, then three or four BBs at eight-inch intervals above that, not forgetting the small shot below the float. The float rig was in fact not too dissimilar from the arrangement I would have used for hemp fishing years earlier; this swim was marginally pacier, but the Thames one was deeper.

While Digby staked out his keepnet in the margins, I assembled his landing net and took the lid off his bait bucket, which held several pints of maggots. Neither of us had a bait apron with us, so I put a good half pint of maggots into one of my coat pockets. With waders rolled up, we were ready to start fishing. We made our way through the low, partially-eaten rushes, leaving the landing net and bait bucket within easy reach. It wouldn't be too difficult to refill my pocket at regular intervals with maggots. It was shallow at the edge with a silvery-coloured silt river bed. As the water deepened further out the silt turned to firm golden gravel, and we stopped at twelve feet out in a depth of two feet.

The swim was special to me and it looked superb. It wasn't suited for bank fishing and waders were essential, while a short line had to be kept between the rod tip and the float to keep in close contact and avoid any bow in the line.

Both banks were used as pasture and a few dead, stunted trees damaged by cattle overhung the water in places. A small stream entered the river twenty yards downstream on the far bank, and as usual there was surprisingly little weed. The area was otherwise featureless except for a large stone or boulder in the middle of the river, the feature which made this the great swim it was. Debris had established itself around the boulder and some branches had been there long enough to root, with leafage just above the surface. The boulder caused the flow to divert around it, creating a slower-paced run.

Before Digby cast to a rod and a half-length to the spot below the stone, I threw in a couple of small handfuls of maggots to get the fish interested. When Digby cast, his float didn't straighten and he was slow to realise that it was already a bite. Although late in reacting, he still managed to hook a fish. His rod tip trembled with its first piscine contact, a nice dace of about seven inches and under three ounces which punched well above its weight. I put the unhooked fish in the keepnet and hoped it would be joined by many others.

More bites and dace did follow, not at every cast, but frequently enough. Then came a more decisive bite, with the float just dipping below the surface; Digby struck into a better fish which offered more resistance. It was a roach, a pristine fish that looked

as if it had just been minted – it weighed about ten ounces, I guessed. Its captor looked very pleased.

I continued to feed maggots, refilling my pocket a couple of times. More dace were caught, then Digby hooked into something much bigger. He had to give line as the fish made off to the far bank. The rod buckled over even more as whatever was on the line swam off downstream and thrashed about in the tail of the swim. We could see it was a chub. I fetched the landing net and we both waded nearer to the fish, where I netted it at the first attempt. At about three and a half pounds it was the biggest fish of the day so far, and it joined the others in the keepnet.

There were by now a couple of dozen or more fish in the net and Digby really seemed to be enjoying his day. After four more fish, Digby thought it a good juncture to have a break for something to eat. He offered me some of his smoked salmon sandwiches and coffee, but I suggested perhaps I could go for a walk to a local pub twenty minutes' walk away. I thought my guest could do with some time to himself, and I think he appreciated that. I rolled my waders down, took the camera from my bag and said I'd be back shortly.

The pub was at least a mile away, but I wanted to stop for a while on the way to look at a side stream where there used to be a few dace, chub and the odd big redfin. I still had at least half a pint of maggots in my coat pocket, and from a narrow bridge spanning the stream I threw in a dozen or so to attract fish. None appeared, not even a dace or a minnow, which was disappointing. The stream appeared totally devoid of fish. Five lifeless minutes passed and I continued on my way to the pub.

Arriving at the pub, I pulled my waders most of the way up and rolled my trousers over the top. It didn't feel particularly comfortable, but at least I wouldn't look out of place. In the bar I bought a pint of draught Irish stout and a sumptuous pork pie. One table was free, and I put my coat on the bench seat and began to enjoy my tasty pie garnished with plenty of mustard. The pub had a faux rustic ambience, was favourably decorated and looked interesting, but it lacked the originality and charm that only an old, stark yet genuine country inn would once offer. I guess it was a sign of the times and pubs needed to modernise.

I polished off my snack and fiddled with the settings on my camera whilst I supped my pint. Once finished and fortified, I put my coat on and left. Outside I could roll down my waders, which were becoming uncomfortable, and set off to return to Digby land.

I couldn't help making the slight diversion to look at the stream again and stopped at the bridge. Once more there wasn't a fish in sight. Perhaps some more bait might work this time, but crikey, my pocket was empty save for five or six maggots. Where had they all gone? I'd lost a whole half pint of them. Then it suddenly dawned on me – they must have escaped from my pocket in the pub. Good heavens! Well that was one boozer I would have to avoid for a long time.

Feeling a little hot under the collar, I carried on to the river, wondering how Digby was getting on. Would he have caught a few more dace or another roach?

Over the stile, I began to cross the meadow feeling flushed from the embarrassment of my stupidity, and the cumbersome waders and warm coat were beginning to slow me down. Over the last rise I could see Digby's tackle but there was no sign of him – well, not at first. As I got nearer I could see him lying on his back, on top of the rushes. Good grief, had he been taken ill? All sorts of thoughts ran through my mind as I raced towards him, feeling hotter and hotter in the process. Would he need help? I didn't have a mobile phone at the time and I didn't know if Digby had one either. Perhaps I would have

to run to the nearest building to phone for help, but there was only the odd farm building some way off, the only place I would be sure to find a phone was – um – the pub. It was twenty minutes away, but how would I be greeted by the landlord with three or four hundred maggots crawling over his seats and carpet?

The last twenty yards to Digby seemed like an eternity – it was like running the last six miles of a marathon. He looked up as I reached him, and appeared to be on the point of laughter. He explained what had happened. He had been wading and catching a few more fish when suddenly a grey torpedo-like thing had brushed by him. He had taken a couple of quick steps back, lost his momentum and started falling backwards, ending up on the rushes. As I helped him to his feet I told him it must have been a pike – it had happened to me in the same swim, when I had previously had a pike swim between my waders as I was fishing. Digby was none the worse for his misadventure, which must have occurred moments before I reached the last rise. He was quite happy in fact, because having caught some more dace he had then landed a good roach, which he thought must have weighed a pound and a quarter at least. His rod was still in the water, and I picked it up and reeled in. A dace was on the end of the line. It showed signs of having been taken by a pike, and I unhooked it and let it gingerly swim off; it had lost a few scales, but at least it was alive.

Digby invited me to try his rod for ten minutes while he went for a walk and to answer the call of nature. The rod indeed was great, and using two of the fresh maggots left in my pocket I cast out. On the second trot down I had a tentative bite which I connected with. It was a decent fish, and I shortly brought a fine redfin to the net – it must have weighed a pound and a half. I unhooked it and released it into the current. Digby returned a few minutes later and asked what I thought of the rod. I told him it was a very fine rod and that he'd made a great choice.

Digby started to fish again, and as I went to feed some maggots I remembered my pocket was empty and I would have to refill it. I made no mention of the escapees in the pub.

More dace followed for Digby and two more roach, nice fish of either side of the pound mark. We had another break mid-afternoon and a coffee as Digby told me a little more about his past military service, without giving too much detail. Back in the river, he continued trotting his float (or rather, my float). He chatted more about his past and said that although now retired, he still didn't have too much time to go fishing. But I felt people like Digby never entirely retire.

We fished on with just one more brief early evening break; Digby by then had a good net of fish, probably getting on for thirty pounds. He had another roach, one of about eight ounces, which looked splendid with its silvery white flanks gleaming in the now descending sun. Bites began to peter out and with sunset expected at 8:30 I knew Digby wouldn't want to fish on for much longer. A few more trots down and the float didn't waver, but then on the next cast, which would have probably been the last of the day, there was a bite at the tail of the swim. Digby struck and was into a better fish. The cane rod bent in response and the fish, certainly too big to be a dace, danced about on the river bed. Wading further out with the landing net I could see it was a roach, a very good one. It dived and surfaced two or three times and finally tired and was guided into the net. Digby couldn't help but yell out a "yes!"

I carried the redfin to the bank and unhooked it as Digby hurried to fetch his weighing scales and net. I passed his prize catch to him so he could admire and weigh it. In the dampened weigh net the roach was put on the scales, which flickered between 2lb and 2lb 1oz. Digby was overjoyed, and I took a

few quick pictures of him cradling his roach before he returned it straight back into the water. Digby couldn't stop smiling; it was his first two-pounder. His day was complete and he was ready to pack up and leave.

As he put his gear away I released the keepnet of its inmates, which all swiftly swam off. With everything packed away, we rolled down our waders and journeyed back to the car park and the waiting Sam sitting in the limo. With the car loaded, we set off, but not before I had made sure my coat pocket was emptied of maggots!

On the trip back I promised Digby I would forward the pictures of him as soon as I could. In response he slipped his business card into my top shirt pocket along with a few notes and gratefully thanked me for showing him the swim. I graciously accepted the gratuity, without checking the amount. Sam dropped me off at home and Digby carried on to his hotel in Bournemouth. He was due to fly home the next morning, not on a scheduled flight but in his own plane!

The next morning I made a quick breakfast, at the same time half watching the local news on the television. Some story about hysteria in a familiar pub caused by an 'infestation' grabbed my attention.

But enough of the telly, I had to go to work. Before setting off, I found the notes and Digby's card still in my other shirt pocket. I read the business card. The letters behind Digby's name were not a surprise, but the 'Sir' in front of it certainly was.

Digby is a great character, a man of many parts, including being the author of many books and well connected. Does he have a plane? Of course not – he has two! Unfortunately I've lost contact with him, because he moved abroad and I lost his address when I moved house. Perhaps one day I'll track him down.

The swim in the story is one of my favourites on the Avon. I have always caught roach from it, though they have been outnumbered by dace, and I have usually had a chub on the day. The last time I visited it, I arrived with a big bucket of maggots at first light, the start time for entry onto the fishery. Two unoccupied cars were already in the car park, and as described I crossed the stile and made my way across the meadow to the river. To my huge disappointment an angler was already fishing in the swim. I returned to the car and fished somewhere else, though from memory I can't recall where. I have never returned to the 'Digby Swim', though I still have a photo of it, for memory's sake.

BIG ROACH

⎯⎯∘⎯⎯

A big roach might be thought of as a good roach, but any roach is a good roach. A two-pound redfin was once a two-ounce fish. Few roach get to reach a large size, and when they do they become very wily fish and one of the most difficult species to catch.

Some stillwaters do regularly turn up big redfins, but they are a captive audience and bear no comparison to catching a big roach from a river, which is a real challenge.

I do have a passion for catching big roach and I have had the good fortune to catch some and witness a few caught by other anglers. Over the years I have also seen other big redfins in the rivers I fish, but I have either failed to catch them or have been unable to fish there.

On one stretch where I fished for roach a number of times, the river keeper told me of some good roach he had seen, but unfortunately no fishing was allowed in the area. I had a look for them one day. It was late autumn and the river was still clear, but fish spotting was difficult because of the angle of the sun and the nature of the far bank, which darkened the surface. The water seemed to have a green tinge, but I'm sure it was an illusion caused by the far bank foliage and the wavering eel grass. Even the stones on the bottom appeared greenish, but I'm sure they weren't. They looked to be worn flat by years of continual water erosion, and I suspected the river bed had changed little over the centuries. I could almost imagine a Roman centurion at the helm of a sea-going boat bound for Salisbury.

It can sometimes take a while for the eyes to be accustomed to the light of the river and for it to slowly begin to reveal its secrets. The eel grass was becoming definable, as was every stone on the river bed. As yet there were no signs of fish. Perhaps the roach were no longer there, but then I saw a triangle of darker colour amongst the weed which moved in the current, and then I made out the shape of a partially-hidden fish, and could see that it was a roach. It looked hardly different in colour to the weed and tinged water, although in reality it would have been a varied palette of colours, highlighted by bright red fins.

As my angle of vision widened I saw another roach, then another, then more, their presence in each case revealed only by their outlines and dark fins. There must have been at least twenty roach in all, many, if not all, over two pounds.

The Kennet has a reputation for big roach in some areas, although I've never caught a decent one from the river – good barbel, chub, grayling and dace, yes, and a few pike. I'm always on the lookout for fish in all locations. One day when I was fishing the Kennet for barbel with my friend Phil, we stumbled upon a tiny feeder stream running across a field. It was barely a trickle in most places except for one bend, where, although surrounded by undergrowth, there was a reasonable depth. We actually had some nice chub from the bend and lost one or two bigger fish which shed the hook.

One summer's day I wandered along this tiny brook with an Avon rod and bait bucket in hand. The rill was barely two yards wide, half that in places, and only inches deep. At one point it deepened to two feet at the most and for about six feet it was weed free. I spotted a few small fish and I thought, why not fish for them with the float tackle and a single maggot?

The small float would only stay in the short trickle for a few seconds before I had to lift it out and drop in again at the head of the gap. I started to catch the small fish, roach, dace and chub, all about the same size and very little discernible difference between the species at first glance. None were big but it was fun fishing, just sitting on the grassy bank on a pleasant sunny day.

Mike Rice's huge Avon roach

As the float reached the end of the trot before coming into contact with the weed, I lifted it out of the water to recast and at the same time a roach glided through the gap and into the weed and out of sight. It was huge, and I stared into the water in disbelief. I never saw it again; serendipity had failed me by seconds. Was it an apparent "big fish in a small pond" misjudgement in the absence of verification, or was it in reality a massive roach?

On the Dorset Stour, I recall that it is often roach that catch my attention the most. In the summer months I rove, feeding swims with hemp and sweetcorn, and often barbel, chub and roach all appear in the swim. It is the roach I want to catch. In one swim I baited all three species appeared, plus what appeared to be some dace, in addition to a fair-size eel which was already present. The chub were a good size, but not big. The barbel may have been six pounds or more and the roach were very big, certainly well over two pounds.

To try and catch the roach, I float fished with a small loafer and a single grain of corn as bait, regularly feeding the pacey swim with small handfuls of mixed hemp and corn. Rather than watching the float I watched the hookbait, which I could see in the clear water. The roach and chub fed mid-depth on the freebies whilst the barbel searched the river bed. But could I get a bite? At first, I could not. The occupants of the swim were keen on the loose bait, but not the corn on my hook.

Eventually I did get a bite. I'd lost sight of which grain of corn had my hook in it, but I saw my float slide under at the tail of the swim and was into a good fish. Somehow it was difficult to bring it to the surface, but after several minutes I did manage to bring it up and it was a huge roach. Unfortunately I could see that I had foul-hooked it in the dorsal fin, which explained the added resistance. Several times it dived down again in the current; I simply couldn't bring it to the net. Ultimately the hook pulled out and the roach swam off. I had no regrets about the loss as I don't like to foul-hook fish, which happens on rare occasions. It would have been interesting to know the weight of the lost redfin though.

I also missed out on another big roach on the same stretch. Again I had baited an area with hemp and corn and float-fished corn in a short run-up to an overhanging willow tree, which I had partly climbed. A very big roach glided through the gap feeding on the sinking freebies, but I never got it to take a bait and I never saw it again on subsequent visits.

One day fellow Barbel Catchers' Club member John Medlow and I were viewing a fishery on the Hampshire Avon for which we had just gained membership. Below a weir we saw a good-sized roach just where it shouldn't have been, alone in a sheltered spot below a weed bed. It looked lost. This was many years ago and I certainly remember it being sizeable. I wonder if John recalls it.

It was not the biggest roach I have seen on the Avon however – that was in the close season on my local stretch of river. The Avon had been severely flooded for weeks and still was. It was still coming off the river and across the fields; the nearby houses still had water in their back gardens. On the higher ground of the riverbank, debris marked the highest point of the flood level and nearby there was a stranded dead roach. It was in perfect condition apart from the head, which was partly eaten. I've never seen such a huge redfin, and it had the biggest and most defined scales I have seen on a roach; it was a sad sight to see the demise of such a giant of the species, but no fish is immortal. Upstream was the stretch that had accounted for big roach up to 3lb 10oz, and it could well have been one of those. It looked that sort of weight.

One roach I would have liked to have seen was caught by my good friend Mike Rice, who was

Records Officer in the Barbel Catchers when I was in the club. Mike often stayed at my place with his mate Chris when they used to fish the Avon. On one visit Mike asked if I could recommend a good area of the Avon to fish for barbel, and I suggested one stretch that was producing some big barbel and said that if he tried feeder fishing with maggots, there was a good chance of picking up a good roach as well. Mike was quite happy that evening. He hadn't caught a barbel but had landed an amazing 3lb 8oz roach, a fish of a lifetime.

BIG ROACH LIST

The record roach is a little over the four-pound mark. We now need a DNA test to fully verify the true identity of the species, which creates two problems: firstly, there is the practicality of obtaining a test and secondly, there is no way of verifying past captures. I see no reason for the elimination of record roach caught in the past simply because they cannot now be identified by modern scientific techniques.

Ray Clarke stunned the angling world with his massive 4lb 3oz roach from the Dorset Stour on the 27th October 1990, which was subsequently regarded as the record. In 2006, Keith Berry caught a 4lb 4oz roach from a Northern Ireland stillwater, and this became the new record. However, some lists still show Ray's 4lb 3oz fish as the record, whilst others accept Keith's fish. I understand that Keith's roach was fully authenticated, so I guess that is the fish to be regarded as the UK record. It appears Keith is no stranger to big roach, having caught a few other very big redfins as well as the record. One would assume that they all came from the same stillwater in Northern Ireland. The 4lb 4oz roach looked truly huge in the photo in *Anglers' Mail*; not only was the fish in perfect condition but it was of immense proportions and showed little sign of being in spawn. Moreover it looked properly 'roachy'.

There have been many roach over the four-pound mark reported, but 4lb 4oz does seem the weight to beat. Quite possibly one has been caught an ounce or two over the record and not authenticated, which is regrettable, but at least the angler will have the personal satisfaction of knowing what he has achieved, and that has to be the overriding sentiment.

It is interesting to note that the vast majority of big roach have come from stillwaters, no doubt having reached their optimum weight from feeding on highly nutritious bait intended for carp. Three fisheries in particular feature at the present time, notably the lakes at the picturesque Linch Hill Fishery in Oxfordshire, which is a highly prolific big carp water. Roach to four pounds have been reported there. I believe there is some day ticket fishing available at Linch Hill. The second water is Highbridge Lakes in Norfolk, which I understand is syndicated. An array of big roach up to 4lb 1oz have been caught from Highbridge and it is no surprise to find that this fishery too is a noted big carp water. Thirdly there is Homersfield Lake in Suffolk, which has recently produced a massive 4lb 3oz roach along with a string of three-pounders. Homersfield sounds a spectacular fishery with carp over fifty pounds, as well as huge tench, bream and big perch. This lake is also syndicated, but I believe it can be fished by booking the holiday lodge on site. Possibly we might see a new record roach from one of these stillwaters, especially if a big spawn-bound one is caught.

A new river record roach is far less likely, I believe. Some have been caught to about four pounds from the Hampshire Avon this century, but achieving those extra few ounces to reach a record would be extraordinary. It also has to be remembered that roach probably reach their peak weight as a result of being in spawn in the close season period on rivers. There is no comparison between a highly-prized big river roach and a stillwater one. A big river redfin is such a rarity - just try and catch one!

Picture and cased cast of Ray Clarke's 4lb 3oz record roach on display in Davis Tackle, Christchurch. Photograph taken by permission of shop proprietor Nigel Gray.

IN GENERAL

WEATHER AND FISHING

If the wind blows from the east the fishing shall cease, if the wind blows from the west the fishing is at its best and so on… well, it might have some relevance but only in a minor way, for many other factors need to be taken into account. Wind intensity and temperature, time of year, water temperature, air pressure, water level and cloud cover are some of the many other components that need to be considered. There are no weather conditions that can guarantee that you will have a good day's fishing, nor are there any conditions, no matter how severe, that will certainly mean you will return home fishless. Yet weather conditions are very significant and do play a large part in what we catch.

The biggest impact the weather has is not on the angler but on the fish. Water is the element in which fish live, they need to survive in it, and they need to find food and reproduce. In this nation barbel and roach are not too fussed about higher temperatures, but in extreme cold they will switch off; not that they cannot be caught in cold water, but it becomes that much more difficult. Visit a river on a daily basis and there is always a subtle difference to the water each day, be it a discernible change in the tinge of the water colour, a variance in water level or temperature or a ripple on the surface. On a cold, grey day in winter the river may look equally grey and feel icy when you put your fingers in the water. Likely when you fail to get a bite, you feel the stream is lifeless. Heavy rain will colour the water and possibly encourage the fish to feed, but there may be some run-off from local roads which can add dirt to the water and displease the fish. Go down to the river in autumn and there may be a golden tinge to the river, the colour of weak beer; you may well smile, for the last time it was that colour you had a very good day.

A forecast of a hurricane may well induce the angler to stay indoors, but I have fished in a hurricane with the roar of the wind and violent swaying of the overhead tree branches almost deafening and a little frightening. Tons of weed were being washed downstream in the visibly rising water level and the rod was buckled over by the mass of weed on the line. The howling wind was louder than the sound of the centre-pin ratchet, but I saw the drum spinning like a bicycle wheel. I grabbed the rod to feel a good fish on the end, and somehow managed to land a fine barbel.

We used to be told that September was the month to fish for barbel, a time when the species was at its fighting best and weather conditions were the most favourable. True, it is possibly one of the best months of the year to fish for them, but in reality they can be caught on any day of the season. I have known the frosty nights of autumn to make an early appearance in September, and have struggled to catch at such times.

October can be the best month of the year. The weather may remain fine and barbel and roach begin to feed once the summer's weed growth begins to thin out. It can also be one of the worst months. Cold, wet and windy weather can see the leaves blown off the trees, which are a nuisance, spiralling down the river and a constant magnet to your line in the water, pulling the bait out of position and not to the liking of fish.

Generally November used to be the worst month for both barbel and roach; the weather was invariably cold and dry with the river running cold, clear and low. But recent years have seen milder Novembers and as a result the fishing has been better.

In winter, up to the end of the season, water temperatures become more significant, but yet again there are no hard and fast guidelines. The water temperature in January could be 8°c, a very

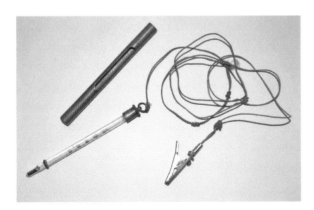

Thermometer with lanyard to crocodile clip for attaching to bankside vegetation

favourable temperature and I would fancy my chances, but it may have been the same for a couple of weeks and a feeding period may have been missed, especially with barbel. A temperature of 6°c may well offer better chances, if it has just risen from a stable 4°c for a couple of weeks. In winter a higher water temperature will on the whole, however, offer the best chances. I like to record both water and air temperature, but a thermometer won't catch you a fish, only a bait in the water will do that.

For roach, any time from autumn onwards is good; a float can be trotted more easily in the less weedy river and fish start to shoal up. The best time has to be the 'back end', when the big redfins show, providing the conditions are mild enough.

So, weather does play a part throughout the year, but there are always fish to be caught. On a bitterly cold winter's day, when the temperature is hovering around zero, why not have a change of tactics and fish a cube of breadcrust or flake for the ever-obliging chub? You may catch a barbel or roach anyway. In sub-zero temperatures why not fish for grayling if you have them in your area? The colder it is, the more they feed.

Cold weather doesn't bother me too much, nor does the heat or even rain, providing it is not heavy, but a strong wind is detestable. It might be okay if I can tuck myself away under the brolly with the wind behind me, and indeed at times I have caught some good barbel in really rough conditions, but no more hurricanes thank you. Nowadays I use a neighbour's flag that can tell me the wind direction and strength. It will tell me which side of the bank to fish from.

A flooded river can be great to fish, especially for barbel. In winter when the river is bank high or in flood, the water is coloured and it is mild, it spells big fish time. Fish the margins and you are in with a great chance of a good fish. It is one of the best times of the year to fish for barbel, and they are

You won't catch a fish watching TV indoors on a cold winter's day – but you might if you go fishing, even at -4 C as I did on this day

heavier too. On the other hand, the river can be in flood with bankside meadows under water and the weather cold; the water can be clear and icy and the run-off from the fields will chill the river. It is not such a good time to fish, but there is always a chance, especially at dusk. Whether it is mild or cold, stealth remains important; you still need to make as little noise as possible. You may want to chat to your mate who is twenty feet away, but the fish can be closer to you than that – avoid anything other than a whisper. The riverbank may be under water, so go prepared with waders and a spare light stool or chair, which is handy to put your rucksack and rod bag on. For roach, I would look for an area of slacker water but not fish where the water is still as the redfins usually like some flow, possibly because of their constant awareness of the threat of pike.

Over recent years we have seen some areas severely flooded, where vast areas of farmland and residential properties have been under water. Fishing on rivers is probably best avoided at such times. Also on a cautionary note, only fish a flooded area if you are familiar with the river, as you need to know exactly where there are ditches and where the riverbank is.

I never intentionally take notice of the weather forecast, whether it is on the radio, on the television or in the press; they all too frequently get it wrong. I learnt that many years ago when the forecast was for a miserable day on the morrow, I stayed at home the next day only to find it a pleasant, sunny day... never again! It is still the case nowadays; the forecasters just get it wrong all too often. The only thing predictable about our weather is that it is unpredictable.

I like to watch the viewers' photos of the daily landscape scenes before the forecast, but beyond that it becomes totally contradictory. The presenter's

150

The Hampshire Avon in full flood at Avon village

forecast differs from the graphics behind them and after that we get the weather again, the national forecast, which gives different temperatures from the local forecast. Change channels on the television and the weather forecast is different again. Not very impressive is it?

For some though, weather warnings need to be heeded. The angler crossing the Pennines, say, or making a long journey, would be wise to listen to local radio stations if there is any kind of weather warning. Otherwise, the only way to see what the weather is doing is to go fishing and look to the sky.

My views on weather forecasting are personal and it would be foolish to suggest my attitude should be adopted by others, who may be well-advised to take notice of forecasts, just pick the most accurate one.

Many people use their mobile phones these days for a forecast, which will be a good option when on the move.

Night fishing

Both barbel and roach will feed at any time of the day. Roach in shoals of small to medium-size fish will often feed all day if they are in the mood, though they prefer the hours of daylight. Bigger redfins are more fickle; they may feed at any time, but only when they really want to. Barbel will also feed at any time, regardless of size. I have found that on unfished or little-fished waters, both species are more inclined to respond to bait almost immediately, but on heavily-fished waters there is a tendency for the feeding times to be more limited. Feeding times can also vary from one water to another but in many cases, big barbel and roach often feed at dawn and dusk.

Fishery rules may dictate that fishing at first light and in fading daylight is not possible, which in some cases is unfortunate. It can be very frustrating to fish all day unsuccessfully for barbel, especially in

the summer and autumn, only to have to pack up just as the sun is beginning to dip below the horizon, just the time when the fish are likely to begin feeding. Fortunately, in many cases nowadays, the start and finish times have been relaxed and the angler is able to fish at first light and into darkness, well into the night on some waters.

When float fishing for roach I usually pack up when I can no longer see the float, by which time it is almost dark. Occasionally I may fish on for half an hour, sliding the float up the line and 'laying on' at close range where I have been introducing groundbait, but by that time I have had enough. Even using quiver tip rods, I still wouldn't fish much more than half an hour into the dark. An afternoon session until dusk for roach, which invariably is in winter, is usually enough to satiate my hunger. Big roach have been caught at night, but they can feed at any time, so I prefer to fish for them in daylight or

fading light. I have caught two-pound-plus roach on the first cast of the day when I could barely see the float and nothing during the remainder of the day, but I prefer afternoons, in winter, that is. Four or five hours' fishing is enough.

Barbel are different. They do feed during the hours of daylight, but dusk is a favourite time, probably the best time of the day to fish. As the sun begins to dip, barbel, like all fish, lose their refractive sight capabilities, become less inhibited and begin to search for food. The angler still needs to keep quiet though, keep well back from the water's edge and avoid sudden movement.

Dusk is a mesmerising time of the day. It is still possible to see, but the landscape begins to lose its definition and colour and as the wind drops, as it often does at this time of the day, quietness descends. The leafless branches, the reeds and rushes no longer rustle and other sounds become more evident; the surface of the water no longer ripples and becomes an apparent flat calm. Fish may begin to pulsate with chub breaking the surface, intercepting floating tasty morsels as they drift downstream. As the minutes quickly pass, it becomes harder to see until there is darkness, when only a slight glint appears on the water and the feeble light on the western horizon starts to fade.

Darkness is a different dimension; it is a different world, one in which the sense of hearing intensifies. Our natural instincts heighten as creatures begin their nocturnal activities, and there is always that tiny element of fear as to what lurks in the blackness of night. Strange things happen at night!

Darkness is not a time for some, and many anglers prefer to pack away their gear and leave as the light fades. That is fully understandable – certainly, if possible, I like to catch fish in daylight, simply because it is nice to see them and appreciate the beauty of their markings and colour. On my favourite and most productive Thames swim, I never caught any of the many barbel in daylight, except for one I caught just as dawn was breaking. Given the choice, I would have rather caught half the number had they been landed in daylight, just so I could have admired them.

I do however really like to fish at dusk and into total darkness. I favour fading light rather than darkness and have caught many of my better fish during that time. For bite detection, once the light has gone, I rely on isotopes whipped onto the rod tip, or I might touch ledger if using one rod.

Tackle organisation is essential at night. I employ the same layout with rod quiver behind the chair, rucksack at my side, a small bait bucket under the chair and the landing net conveniently placed. An unhooking mat can be put under the landing net, or if you've got a folding one like mine, they make a good cushion to sit on. Packing up is simple. I just wind in and snip off the end rigs using the folding scissors from my jacket pocket, which I put in my bait bucket, which goes in the rucksack along with the reels. The sections of the rods go in their bags whilst I am still seated. It just remains for them to then go into the quiver, along with the rod rests and the quick folding landing net. The folded unhooking mat goes into the folded chair. With rucksack and rod quiver on my back I fold my chair, hold it by the foot bar and I'm on my way.

Isotopes waiting to light up at nightfall

I carry two very small torches, which I use as little as possible. One I keep in my jacket pocket and the other, a spare one, is in the side pocket of my rucksack. I don't favour head torches and have never used one, except on a visit to a deep-mined coal face. Many of those who go night fishing for sea trout hang small torches around their necks to ensure they can't lose them. It's best to keep the use of torches to a minimum; switch one off after several minutes use and you will likely become disorientated. Get accustomed to the darkness. If the torch is too bright, paint the lens green or partially cover it with tape.

As with floods, you need to be very familiar with the bankside and the footpath back to the car park. Where there are any wooden plank bridges, exposed tree roots or any other potential hazards, I make a mental note of where they are, counting the number of footsteps from known landmarks to their whereabouts in daylight. The journey back to the car in darkness when the riverbank is under water takes even greater care.

One of my favourite and most familiar swims on the Avon involves a walk back to a friend's cottage on a rise. It doesn't look far but it is a good ten-minute walk, even taking a short cut across the fields rather than following the longer zig-zagging footpath. Often a thick mist descends upon the valley at nightfall, greatly reducing visibility, but that has never been a problem as I know the landscape well.

One night however, a really thick fog developed in the darkness and visibility was almost zero. A torch was of no use and if anything it only made things worse, as I could barely see my boots. After I packed up, I headed in the direction I thought was right and slowly took short steps. That was no good – I was getting nowhere. The only option was to take a rod out of its bag and use it to feel the way ahead. There were fences to negotiate but luckily none were electric and the cattle were in the barn. I eventually came to the first fence that I had been expecting and clambered over it and continued straight on. I was making very slow progress and it was a little eerie not knowing what was ahead of me. Finally I reached the last fence, but behind it was a wood; I'd gone off course. I suspected it was the wood behind the cottage, so I turned right and followed the line of the fence. Thankfully, I came to the stile that I had been aiming for and the gravel path to the cottage was short, straight and easy going. The ten-minute walk had turned into a thirty-minute one and I was relieved to open the front door of the cottage.

When you're fishing at night there are often noises in the undergrowth. They can be caused by all kinds of creatures, but quite often the culprits are rats. It is something you get used to. I've had lots of encounters with Mr. Rattus, the long-tailed rodent, some of them of the close kind. On the Thames I never saw them in daylight but at night there were many afoot, and afoot is exactly where they went, constantly running over my feet. Fortunately I used to wear wellies at the time, so they didn't pose any threat. I even had one on my shoulder once – I'd been lying on my bedchair during the night by the Kennet at Burghfield, waiting for sunrise, and one of the blighters woke me up. It was on my shoulder looking at me. I brushed it off and went back to sleep. A friend fishing on a Thames weir suddenly noticed his coat pocket was jumping up and down and found it was a rat which had taken a fancy to the bag of cheese in his pocket.

One night, on the Kennet again, I heard a rustling sound approaching me. The bank was wooded and I could hear twigs snapping as the creature came closer, so it was definitely no rat. They don't break things as they walk along. The footsteps became louder until the beast was almost next to me – it was a dog, and it sat down beside me, no doubt hoping for something to eat. A couple of chunks of luncheon meat and the canine was on its way. I've often had dogs come and sit beside me, but never before at night. Unbelievably, half an hour later, the same thing happened again – another rustling sound and the snapping of twigs. It was another dog! This one also sat down beside me. After a couple of pieces of luncheon meat, that one too happily continued on its way.

Many things have happened during the hours of darkness, but one of the strangest occurred again on the Kennet. I was fishing an hour after nightfall on a thickly-wooded stretch of the river (not where I encountered the dogs) and I heard the sound of twigs and branches breaking; something was approaching me, and it wasn't human. A huge spectre began to appear in the dim light – it must have been eight feet tall. It's sometimes difficult to make out what is near you in the darkness unless it is close up and I had no idea what this ghost-like thing was. What could it be? It came closer and closer until I began to make out its shape – it was a white horse. What it was doing walking along a thickly wooded riverbank in the dark, I don't know.

Fishing on a riverbank at night which is quite open with just meadows behind, you don't expect to get a sudden blast of air in your left ear, which is what happened to me one night on a local stretch of the Avon. It was as if someone had switched on a hair drier behind me. On turning round I was confronted by the head of a massive stag with huge antlers breathing on me. The monster would have had no trouble pushing me into the river, but fortunately its curiosity was satisfied and it wandered off. Foxes, hedgehogs, squirrels, cows, boats, giant moths, blackbirds, bats, pheasants and shotgun-toting fishery owners, yes, I've encountered all of those by night as well. As I said, things happen at night.

I'm not one for fishing several hours in the dark on rivers, other than when I used to fish the Thames, and usually an hour or so is enough for me. Night fishing is fruitful – a little spooky maybe for some, but it is fun.

A big roach caught by George Morris

155

COLIN'S TOP TIPS

These are some of the reminders – a shortlist of things to remember before setting off for a day's fishing. The first is FAB – not a hip word from the 1960s, but the best acronym I can think of to help you make a final check before setting off.

F is for Food. One of the easiest things to forget – we might get it ready, have it out on the table, then forget it. It is always worth carrying a bottle of water, not a fizzy drink; one can always be left in the car. In the summer it can get hot and I have known someone suffer from sunstroke, a serious condition; water is always worth taking as well as a brimmed hat, which brings me to…

A is for Apparel, clothing that is (FCB doesn't make such a good acronym). This is another essential that is easily forgotten. On a Fenland trip, some time ago, my mate realised halfway down the road that he had forgotten his coat and we had to return for it. You do not go fishing on a cold winter's day without adequate clothing. Colour of clothing? Think green.

B is for bait, easily left in the fridge or freezer or in the garage and forgotten. Also something that is worth keeping permanently in the car, tins of sweetcorn, luncheon meat and pellets. Maybe some feed baits as well, such as a crumb mix, tins of hempseed and so on.

A 'FAB' sign above the front door, or a sticker in the car boot, will act as a reminder for the above.

Always pre-plan your trip, decide exactly where you are going before you set off and even think of swims you are likely to fish. Have a plan B, just in case. You may have particular swims in mind and know the stretch well, but if not, spend as much time as possible walking the banks. A session might be four to twelve hours; it only takes five to ten minutes to hook and land a barbel, even a good one, or a big roach, so make sure you are in the right spot. Always walk upstream when looking for a swim and keep well back from the water's edge. A well-worn bank will suggest a popular swim; bankside vegetation will be less. As the majority of anglers are right-handed, think of fishing left-handed and use whatever natural cover is available. Also think about fishing upstream, as very few anglers do.

Avoid over-feeding a swim – less is best. More bait can always be added if the fish start to feed. For roach in particular, the old adage 'little and often' is totally correct.

Keepnets are okay for roach, but release the fish at the end of the day, without taking the keepnet out of the water.

Big roach are very scarce, and when they do feed, they sometimes have a tendency to take a bait on the drop, so be prepared.

The care of fish

Fish have a tough time of it. Throughout their lives they continually have a struggle against predation from pike and other fish as well as from birds and carnivorous animals. Many won't survive long through natural causes, and others will die from the lack of a sustained food supply or disease. The fish's environment can turn against it; variations in flow can create low water levels, which can deprive them of oxygen or expose them to predators, or flooding, which can leave some fish stranded and unable to return to the river. Weather can also play a part, with reduced oxygen levels in hot weather and food supplies severely reduced during lengthy periods of cold water.

Many fish will never be caught by angling means, while some may be hooked and landed a few times and the bigger fish, especially barbel, will become 'known' and likely to have nicknames. It goes without saying that we as anglers need to take care of all the fish we catch so they can be returned in good condition and health to survive to a good age. That care should equally apply to small as well as large fish for all big fish were once small.

Landing fish

The first consideration has to be getting a fish onto the bank safely. It may not be a problem on a canal or a wide-open river such as the Thames, or a stillwater, but often there may be overhanging trees, snags, a steep-sided bank or a marginal fast flow to contend with. The angler initially has to ask the question, if a fish is hooked, can it be safely landed? You should not hook a fish first, then think about how to get it on the bank. A swim may well hold fish, but if there is any doubt that you will be able to land them from it, move on.

High, steep-sided banks are tricky, especially if they are muddy. I generally try to avoid them and although with an extended landing net handle and outstretched arm I can probably reach twelve feet, I doubt if I would consider having to reach over eight feet. Remember too that a fish has to be returned to the water.

Barbel fight incredibly hard and adequately strong hooks and lines are essential. Eight-pound breaking strain line is about right; 10lb may be deemed preferable in some snaggy swims, but there is a discernible difference in suppleness between the two breaking strains.

It was often the practice of some anglers to use only 4lb line, particularly with feeders, and quite a few fish were landed but some were lost. I see little point in using such a fine line for barbel that you have to tire them to the point of exhaustion before you can land them. Fortunately these days the vast majority of barbel anglers are wiser and better equipped, and it is a long time since I've had to remove small hooks from barbel 'lost' by others.

Once hooked, constant pressure should be applied to a barbel, but it should not be excessive. The aim should be to keep the rod neither too low nor too high. If a fish wants to power off, let it do so. This is where a centre-pin excels, as the right amount of pressure can be applied to the drum. Fixed-spool reel drags don't quite have that same assuredness, not to mention the reduced pleasure in playing a fish. As the fish tires, line can be retrieved until it can eventually be brought to the surface. There will be a point when it can be guided towards the bank and over a submerged landing net. Don't go chasing the fish with the net, as there's a chance of losing it. Keep the rod tip a little higher, but not above the vertical.

Many a photo will show an angler stretching his rod arm backwards and his net arm forwards to get a fish in the net – not the way to do it.

Barbel often become snagged in weed, but usually by employing the right tactics they can be freed and landed. As soon as they become immovable, slowly slacken the line – often that works and the fish will move off. It always helps if the angler can move downstream if the fish is snagged in weed, as that way it can be freed more readily. Moving upstream merely pulls the fish further into the roots of the weed or into the snag. If that tactic fails, slacken off and wait a few minutes. I put the rod in a rest pointed towards the snag and loosen the line. Most times the fish will have freed itself by then, but if not I hold the line with both hands and slowly pull, then increase the pressure. This is more sensitive than holding the rod and feeling the line, and it will give a better idea if a fish is still on. On one occasion, the only way I could land a snagged barbel was to pull it all the way to the waiting net by hand. With such a mass of weed I wasn't sure if the fish was in the net, but it was and a good one too.

Rarely, a fish may be lost and the hook can be embedded in thick roots. The only way to retrieve the hook (the same applies if the rig is caught up in a tree branch by a mis-cast) is to wind the line around a twig, or better still a rod rest, and slowly walk backwards. Holding the line will only cut your fingers. Be prepared for the velocity of the weight when it shoots free. On the Kennet a small Arlesey bomb embedded itself a few inches into the mud by my feet as I pulled it free from a far bank branch. Keep your back to the water to avoid injury.

Roach don't present the same problems, but a very big redfin can exceed the breaking strain of the line. They do put up a good dogged fight for up to a few minutes, so caution is needed.

As already mentioned, I err on the side of a larger landing net, partly because when a fish is hooked at dusk, guiding it to a bigger net offers greater confidence. It is better to drag the net in rather than lifting it. Lifting puts a great deal of strain on the handle of the net.

Unhooking

With the fish in the landing net it is best placed on an unhooking mat or a grassy patch, not on gravel or hard ground. Short curved forceps are best for unhooking barbel; they can firmly grip the bend of the hook. A disgorger is ideal for roach. I have never had a deeply-hooked fish of either species, but on one occasion a nearby angler had difficulty in unhooking a barbel that had swallowed his bait. I was able to help by gripping the flat handle of a disgorger with forceps and sliding it down inside the fish's mouth. It obviously survived, as I caught the same twelve-pounder eighty yards away a year later.

Returning fish

All fish should be returned to the water as soon as possible. If practicable, barbel are best held in a gentle current, not in very fast water. One hand should grip the wrist of the tail with the other supporting the head. Once you feel it has regained its strength, it can be released. If the recovery has been misjudged it should be possible to retrieve the fish and start again, but in fast water it may quickly drift downstream unable to regain its balance.

Gently return roach to the margins by hand if possible. Ideally the hands should be wet, and never use a towel to hold a fish.

Returning a fish by lowering a landing net into the water is fine and it's often the only option, especially if there is marginal weed. A fish placed in the water in the net will visibly regain its strength

after a while and can be safely allowed to swim away by further lowering the net. Never throw a fish back, not even a two-ounce roach – they are not Olympic high-board divers and the impact with the water can damage them.

Weighing and photographing

I've weighed and photographed a good number of fish over the years, but if I can I prefer just to unhook them, admire them and release them. Sometimes however it is interesting to know the weight and to have a memento in the form of a photo. Weighing and photographing is best done kneeling down and transferring the fish to a dampened weigh net, keeping it as near to the ground as possible just in case it slips out.

Photos of prized captures will be much valued by the angler and treasured forever. Pictures should be taken quickly, so always keep the camera handy and not at the bottom of the tackle bag. Make sure the fish is free from dirt and vegetation. There is nothing worse than finding the fish has a leaf on its head when the pictures are viewed later on at home. Kneeling when taking a picture will allow the fish to be lowered to the ground if it becomes lively. Standing up risks dropping a fish.

Roach are notoriously difficult to photograph. They are not big fish and a fistful of fingers on the fish can look ungainly. Two fingers of each hand pinched at each end of a redfin may show just about all of the body and makes a nice picture, but it should be avoided – one flip of the fish and it will fall to the ground. Roach need to be supported in some way.

You can look at the fish or at the camera – either makes a good photo. I prefer the former, as it seems to capture the moment of joy of admiration of the fish by the angler. Looking at the camera appears more like a pose though it will make a good press photo, especially if you smile – so many anglers posing with big fish are frowning as if they have just opened their tax bill!

Flash helps in most cases and is useful even in sunny conditions. A fill-in flash will lighten the shaded areas such as the shadow caused by the angler's hat, and enhance the colour balance of the picture. Whatever camera you're using, try to vary the exposure, to make sure both the angler and the fish are reasonably well exposed. It may help to try the shot from two or three different directions to get the best light, and also to consider how the background may enhance the picture.

Sometimes I have been concerned at the length of time spent by others taking photos. I've felt it necessary to politely interrupt and advise that the fish should be returned quickly to the water. There has been the odd mumbled reply, but I've not been punched on the nose – yet! Try to be helpful to others on the bank rather than critical.

LAST CAST

━━━◦━━━

Having dealt with all that, let's get back to the river one last time. The weir pool I am fishing is one of my favourites; the outlook is idyllic, with a picturesque farmland surround. I've had two or three barbel from the pool in the past but not from the side I am on now.

It doesn't get a great deal of attention, despite a report of a thirteen-pounder once, and today I have it to myself. The barbel I have caught from the weir pool have not been big, except for something unseen I hooked once; a sudden pull on the line was met with solid resistance. Whatever was at the end of the line slowly began to move downstream and I could make no impression on it with my strong barbel gear as it moved along the river bed like a rolling barrel of beer. There was no thumping on the line, just an immovable resistance heading towards the tail of the pool.

It continued on its way until it reached the end of the pool and turned around the next bend, where it came off. Whatever had I hooked? Could it have been a giant barbel or another species, a salmon perhaps (I've seen them in the pool before), or something inanimate like a log? I'll never know. It's not the first time I have hooked into some solid, moving resistance; usually it has been whilst roach fishing, but the 'monster' has moved upstream and come off, and logs don't move upstream!

It reminds me of a fish a friend hooked, also in

a weir pool but not this one. For fifty minutes he played the monster and could make no impression on it; each time it neared the bank, it surged off again with enormous power. With tired arms he eventually, somehow managed to get it into slacker water where he could net it. He was horrified to see that the monster was a large tin, the sort used to carry crisp packets; they were often used years ago to carry a gallon of maggots. Of course, each time the big tin had neared him it would have been carried off by the current. Although disappointed, I guess it was lucky he found out what it was. Had the tin come off, he would have forever thought he'd lost a fish of a lifetime.

I have had no bites today in this pool and with fifteen to twenty minutes left to fish before I must vacate the fishery, this will be my last cast. The bait is a large chunk of luncheon meat the size of an average spectacle lens, the hook is a size 6 and the weight a 1.1 ounce bomb. I always fancy my chances with the last cast of the day, and today is no different – I can just imagine a sharp pull on the line. A gentle swing of the weight and it lands in the white water, close to the sill, just where I want.

The light is fading and the formerly vivid crimson and grey mackerel sky has already turned into a sombre grey, along with the whole landscape, except for the lusty rush of water through the hatches, which offers the only brightness. A few biteless minutes pass and I give the weight a twitch towards me; perhaps a movement of the bait will tempt a barbel. Another five minutes pass and I repeat the ploy. Will the last few remaining minutes be eventful, or fruitless?

Well, as it happened that weir pool session was a blank, but no matter, I'm back on the river today, only this time the roach are the target. Again, with fifteen minutes remaining, I make my real last cast of the day. I really fancy a good roach from the swim, but this is my third session in the same spot and

I've only caught one, an eight-ounce fish. Avon roach fishing just isn't easy.

The swim has all the ingredients to hold some redfins; there are tall reeds in the margins, bankside cover behind and a steady flow with uniform depth. Actually I have had a good afternoon, the eight-ounce roach mentioned and a few chub, which provide great sport using the float with a fine line. They are not big chub, but I have caught them on each occasion I've fished the swim. Why others don't fish it I have no idea. Although the fishery is supposedly noted for its roach fishing, rarely have they made an appearance, as I have discovered when I've chatted to the other regulars at the end of the day in the car park.

I've already put some dark tubing on the float tip, so I can just make out the float in the increasing gloom. The crystal Avon float lands just short of mid-river on this narrow stretch, where the river has divided some distance upstream. Bait, as usual, is bread flake on a size 12 hook.

The float travels on its journey down the swim, which I've been baiting all afternoon. It doesn't dither as it drifts into the slacker water of the margins, but then seconds later it dips under and I strike and connect with a fish. It's yet another chub, which makes for the reed stems in the margins. I dare not let it get into the reeds for I will surely lose it, so I bully it perhaps a little more than I should with the 2.4lb line, but the 13ft rod, although crisp in action, is forgiving. The fine line is thankfully dependable and the chub yields.

I coax it towards the middle, where it fights on for a couple of minutes. I can feel it tiring and it begins to rise to the surface, where – crikey, it has red fins! It's a roach, and a big one. And to think I've been pushing the line to its limit! Gratefully I ease the redfin towards the safety of the net, where I leave it to rest while I quickly ready the scales and weigh net and mount the camera and flash on a bank stick.

The roach looks bigger than I thought as I lift it onto the bank and unhook it. It weighs two pounds eight ounces, by no means my biggest but nonetheless a corker to land on the last cast. Some pictures are taken with the Nikon and I safely return the roach to the swim. Tackle quickly gathered, I briskly walk to the car park so I'm visibly off the fishery. I've often been blessed with a good fish on the last cast of the day, quite often it has been a nice barbel, but this redfin has to be the best.

It is not only the last cast that is memorable; the 14th March certainly is, as is the start of the season, which is always eagerly awaited on the river. Year-open stillwaters, although great to fish, somehow lack that sense of seasonality that rivers provide. I really hope the close season on our rivers will remain forever.

Memorable days can often involve just one incident, something unusual or strange, not necessarily the capture of a fish or even fish-related. Many an angler who has spent a good number of days (and nights) by the waterside will have his own stories to tell, be it of things that go bump in the night or strange occurrences they have witnessed. Some may well have witnessed strange things in the sky; shooting stars are common, as are double rainbows (in daylight). The International Space Station and comets may have been seen and even a UFO – in fact I have seen one myself. It was a metallic, diamond-shaped object which remained stationary for quite a while, and I have also had the good fortune to witness a hint of the Aurora Borealis years ago, when fishing a north-facing bank.

Animals common and rare, birds, moths and other creatures are often seen, and sometimes they are recognisable, other times not. When I was once working in the conservation department of a local authority on a local hilltop, a colleague, an ornithologist, told me one day that there were six different types of raptor in the thermals above, yet I could spot none. Slowly as I peered through his binoculars I could make out tiny black shapes circling above. Buzzards and kestrels I know as well as well as sparrowhawks, which wiped out all the house sparrows in my garden. I even had one come and land by my side whilst fishing, so close I could have touched it. Kingfishers are adorable and I've had them land on my rod a few times as I've been holding it. The first time was on the Kennet, when I saw the unmistakable blue of a bird as it flashed by. I thought it would be wonderful if it flew back and landed on my rod, and it did. Many of the wingers I see I don't know the names of, but the beauty is in their admirable colouration and flight, not their names. Butterflies, moths, dragonflies and

damselflies are equally exquisite. I had a huge moth once which took a liking to my car boot and refused to leave as I packed my gear away in the darkness. Naturally it started to fly around me as I was driving home – in retrospect it might even have been a bat.

I tend not to watch the countryside and natural history programmes on the television too much, because although the photography is tremendous and the creatures enthralling, I've seen it all for myself. The animals I see are native to our kingdom, and not only can you see them, you can hear them, and sometimes smell or even touch them. The increasingly rare hedgehog I have picked up and moved to safer locations. Rabbits are so common in some places that they are too numerous to count, and the buzzards above will be looking for them; they form a large part of their diet. Horses take a liking to me and my tackle, probably looking for some food. One put his head in my rucksack and the daft thing couldn't get out of it. It was amusing to watch it running around the meadow behind me with my bag on its head, but not so funny trying to find the scattered contents in the long grass.

Cows have often featured on my days on the riverbank, which are often on farmland. Once I found a dead new-born calf in my swim as I arrived at dawn. After an hour or two, the membrane-covered bovine started to come to life; it began to stumble to its feet and was joined by its mother. Nothing compares to the real-life experiences.

Bulls like to chase me, but they have yet to catch me. They are clever chaps – they wait until you are half-way across their field and then begin to make their charge. I just managed to dive to safety over a fence on one close encounter. I have rescued dogs which have been miles off course, but it wouldn't have surprised me if they knew exactly where they were, they have such a strong homing instinct. One mischievous canine even made off with a small fish I'd just caught on the Thames, and with tail wagging it even came back for more, though its request was denied.

Some very odd things have happened when I've been fishing, and oddly it's nearly always been when I have been pike fishing, so really they don't belong in this book, but why not just a couple? The most bizarre thing happened one winter's day when I was after pike on a pit at Burghfield. The day was cold but the sun had some warmth in the still, cloudless sky. I was quite happy togged up with my thermals on and a big flask of coffee by my side. I only had a few sprats for bait, so I used one rod with an air-injected bait, fished just above the bottom. I had a run and after a few seconds tightened into a fish, a medium-sized pike, which was easily landed. The pike had a treble hook in its mouth along with a fifteen-inch trace and a swivel at the end and no line attached, but it wasn't my hook. Where was my hook? It was through the eye of the swivel that was at the end of the trace already attached to the pike! The sprat had come off in the fight. It sounds impossible, but it happened. I freed the pike of the hook and trace that it had been carrying around for how long I don't know and returned it back to the water, all for the better.

I've digressed, so back to the roach. One day I was on a fenland trip for pike, along with a bit of roach fishing on the float. The fenland drain I was fishing with a mate was very remote. Usually the water was still or slow-moving, but occasionally

Father and son roach fishing at Iford Bridge

the nearby pumping station would release water, no doubt floodwater from the Great Ouse. This floodwater would cause the drain to flow and top its banks, leaving pools of water on the bank as the level dropped. Most of the pools had dried up or dropped in level on our arrival, with only three remaining.

On the dry land there were dead minnows, loads of them. It was surprising they hadn't been eaten by the numerous birds in the area. I picked one up; it was bent like a curved banana, its skin wrinkled and crisp, dried out by the biting easterly wind. The motionless eyes pointed upwards; it was clearly as dead as Monty Python's parrot. I tossed it into the clear drain and it fluttered down like a coin in a fountain, only more slowly. Perhaps a pike, zander or perch might seize it, but no. Then I was sure I could see a movement in the minnow - and seconds later it wriggled and swam off. It had come back to life.

Naturally I then had to pick up all the others and throw them in the drain, and in every case the same thing happened; they all came back to life. I don't know if it is a commonly known phenomenon, but it certainly surprised me. I did consider throwing some fish fingers into my local harbour, but on second thoughts that would have been a resurrection too far…

Nothing really weird has occurred whilst roach fishing, other than a redfin leaping onto the bank. Unsurprisingly, pike have grabbed roach as I have been retrieving them and one toothy rascal had the audacity to swim between my waders and seize one just as I was about to grasp it in the water.

Barbel, as I wrote before, tend to live on the river bed, but they do move up to the surface sometimes, like the minnow-chasing big barbel I have mentioned and the Kennet barbel feeding upside down on the surface. Barbel love feeders and it wasn't uncommon for them to grab maggot-filled ones on the drop, often resulting in them being foul-hooked in the chin.

They love small bait droppers too, or at least their contents, and have often grabbed them as well.

Barbel are nosey too. At the start of one eagerly-awaited season, I opted to fish for them locally on what I hoped would be a quiet area, and indeed that proved to be the case, with not a single angler in sight. There was no swim as such, just tall, thick, lush rushes along the margins. I was at the top of the stretch where the river divided and on my side, the stream was narrower and took less of the flow. It was possible someone could have chosen to fish the upstream-facing point opposite, about thirty feet away, but I had never seen anyone fishing the small pool, no larger than a square yard on the edge of a very fast current. I had fished there myself once and caught a six-pounder, but didn't feel it was worthy of much attention. My aim was to fish right in the margin, which was barely three feet deep. There was a clear, clean gravel run along the edge beyond the rushes and I anticipated a barbel (or two) might patrol the run.

To create a gap in the tall rushes, I lowered my landing net sideways, then laid it flat so it would give a parting just wide enough to fish from. At the end of the day I could lift the net and the rushes would straighten and give no indication of anyone having fished the spot.

I used one rod, and the tip hardly reached the water's edge as I sat well back to avoid being seen or heard. The bait was sweetcorn, a great early-season bait for barbel, and I fished a couple of kernels on a hair and lowered a couple of droppers full of corn and hemp onto the bottom. Cattle were grazing in the field behind me (fortunately they hadn't eaten the rushes, probably because of a steep gravel slope along the bank). The slope looked unnaturally uniform and lacked vegetation; no doubt the area had seen some sort of landscaping in recent times to improve the bank's stability.

My Adjusta chair coped perfectly with the steep slope and it was a pleasure to be back on the bank again, on what was a very pleasant day. The only person in sight was a farmer in a distant hay meadow, driving his tractor. Just being by the water was pleasurable enough and any barbel would have been a bonus. I did catch one, a fine golden bronze and white specimen over eight pounds, which took my bait with a savage bite after a few hours' fishing.

The gap in the rushes was wide enough to give a good view of the water and the luxuriant water crowfoot, wavering in the current, was fascinating to watch. The long strands of the ranunculus would sway from side to side, sometimes come to a standstill, then wave with vigour, even disappearing under the surface as the water sped up in disharmony with the weed upstream. There were gaps at the tail of each weed bed, but they were not wide enough to fish a bait as the roots of the ranunculus covered much of the river bed.

I watched as the water crowfoot was pushed underwater by the surface flow for perhaps a minute, and then as it returned to the surface, I saw that a barbel was lying on the top. It was just resting on the weed, supporting itself by its pectoral and pelvic fins, and I was so close to it that I could see its eyes swivelling. I honestly believe it had come to the surface to take in the surrounding landscape, as it was looking all around, viewing everything in sight.

Eventually the surface water speeded up and the weed and the barbel disappeared from sight. A little later the weed was back on the surface, as was the barbel, still looking around. Then the weed dropped and reappeared a third time, but now the barbel had gone.

Barbel regularly feed on all the popular baits, maggots, corn, pellets and boilies, but sometimes they favour only one of them. There was one day that my mate Ray will probably remember well. A guy was fishing a popular swim; he started early morning using maggots in conjunction with a feeder, which is often successful in the swim. Biteless by lunchtime, he moved to the next good swim, 25 yards downstream. Ray came along and fished the now vacant swim, and in half an hour he had three barbel on trundled meat, then left the swim to give it a rest and wandered downstream. The frustrated, fishless angler returned to the swim for a while and again failed to get a bite. After a spell he returned to his other swim, leaving the popular swim vacant again. I arrived shortly after and finding the hot spot vacant, had a try with meat. I also had three barbel in a short time and like Ray, moved off downstream to rest the swim. The hapless angler must have been staring daggers at me each time I landed a fish, and when I moved on, he never returned to the now vacant swim. Barbel simply didn't have an appetite for maggots on that day.

It is amazing what gadgetry the angler has at his or her disposal nowadays. All these devices are compact and will fit in a pocket or in a rucksack. Miniature waterproof cameras can now be cast to the vicinity of your hookbait and video-played on a smartphone. Mobile phones list all sorts of apps useful to the angler, including one detailing the topography of the river or lake bed, other data and, of course, the weather. Fish-finders can not only be used from a boat but from a rod tip now, I believe.

Some say these gadgets are cheating – they are not that, but I believe they are totally against the spirit of angling. Angling is all about watercraft, knowledge of fish behaviour, patience, adventure and the mysticism as to what lurks near to where we have placed our baits – the unknown. A mobile phone might prove useful in the case of an emergency, but otherwise they are best turned off on arrival at the waterside. There is nothing worse than hearing a ringtone on the bank, especially in the dark, and enduring loud, pointless conversations.

There was once a device on the market that would strike whenever there was a bite – an auto strike. It was fixed to the rod in front of the handle and would respond to a pull on the line, another contraption that is best assigned to the bin. We have self-hooking set-ups nowadays, anyway – they are called bolt rigs or fixed weights. Such fixed weights play no part in my fishing; some fisheries ban them, and I would do likewise if I had my own fishery.

It is pleasing to see young anglers and beginners on the bank. I see some youngsters with their parents, which is great to see, as it reminds me of my childhood. These youngsters are the mature anglers of the future. There does, however, appear to be a dearth of older teenagers and young adults on the bank. Sure, there are some on commercial stillwaters, but few on the rivers. Where they are out of school or university term time is a mystery. I never see them either on my local beaches, where there are plenty of youngsters and adults. I guess some will have part-time jobs but hopefully not many will be at home playing TV games, hardly a healthy pastime.

Angling is a healthy outdoor hobby and should be enjoyed by all. Clubs often have open days for juniors and beginners, and tackle shops will have details about these, or there are many coaches available who are qualified and probably insured. It's a good way to get started. Fishing is not about sitting in the rain all day not catching anything and getting bored. It is about being outdoors. Some days may be rainy, others sunny, and it may be cold or warm – you just take the weather as it comes and take appropriate clothing. It is about enjoying the flora and fauna, making lifelong friends and enjoying social events. Fish, to some extent, are a bonus; the sight of a vanishing float, a rod tip bending round or a bite indicator jumping into life are all wondrous thrills. Get it right, which may not happen at first, and you will find a handsome fish at the end of the line. Fishing is very addictive – catch one fish and you can't wait for the next, or the next day by the water's edge.

The novice only needs to start with humble beginnings; a six-inch roach or two from a pleasant canal will be much enjoyed. It is all part of a learning curve, because bigger fish will follow later. Fishing is not a matter of life and death, but it is more compelling than any other sport or pastime.

Well, it is almost time to put my Lamy pen down and finish writing. It has taken far longer than I envisaged when I first began to draft this book. In fact I've moved house in the meantime. I still live in Christchurch, but now in a quieter location; the garden is bigger and I have finally installed the pond that I've always wanted. Usually the only noise is from ducks quacking on a small lake behind, and they sometimes visit the pond. The latest addition to the pond is a thirty-pounder, a lovely black and red fan-tailed fish. Watching the fish is very therapeutic and I look after them, though a heron recently somehow managed to get one out through the netting. That's why I bought a new one, which, yes, cost thirty pounds.

I sincerely hope you have found my book interesting and hope that whether you are a newcomer or an old hand, it may have inspired you to cast a line. I wish all my fellow anglers many happy days fishing, and with good fortune I'll meet you on the bank.

Tight lines!

INDEX

Printed in Great Britain
by Amazon

55454496R00104